In Fear of
AFRICAN
AMERICAN
MEN

JUSTINE RECTOR

To: Mr & Mrs Askins

Best Wishes

Justine Rector

3/23/03

2002, Second printing
Second edition expanded

Published by Justine Rector
4429 Sherwood Road – B-2
Philadelphia, PA 19131
215-473-3714 tel/fax
215-473-0234 fax
teenieweenie1947@yahoo.com
http://www.tinetor8m.com

Library of Congress Catalog No. 98-92103

ISBN: 0-9667366-1-3

Printed in the United States of America

Since 1975, Professor Justine Rector has researched, written, lectured and held conferences as a pioneer asking the question "Are African American Males an Endangered Species???," *In Fear of African American Men, The Four Fears of White Men* resulted from those endeavors.

Professor Rector, an African American native of Philadelphia, Pennsylvania, has a Bachelor of Arts in History, University of Pennsylvania, and a Master of Science in Journalism, Columbia University; post graduate studies at Howard University and the University of Pennsylvania, and has an ND degree in Naturopathic Medicine.

She retired from Howard University where she was an Associate Professor of Journalism in the School of Communications; formerly she was a Journalism instructor in the School of Communications and Theater, Temple University, and currently is an adjunct professor in Community Services and English at the Community College of Philadelphia. She is also a lecturer in alternative health.

Professor Rector did free lance reporting for the Washington Post, the Washington Star, the Philadelphia Inquirer, the Philadelphia Tribune, the Philadelphia New Observer and has written journal articles. She reported for the Pacifica National News Bureau, co-anchoring with Julian Bond the 20th Anniversary March on Washington; consulted and did research for radio and television stations in Los Angeles and Washington, D.C.; hosted "Third World View," Ch. 6, Philadelphia, Pa.; co-authored *Issues and Trends in Afro American Journalism*. She held earlier positions in City government and law enforcement.

She is a community activist and for many years a member of numerous political, social, civic and educational organizations.

Dedication

Dedicated to the memory of William "Bill" R. Meek, mentor, role model, and faithful friend. He was a courageous, life-long warrior and advocate for freedom and justice for people of all cultures. "You must finish this book" were his last words spoken to me.

Written with the fervent hope for the survival of great-grandsons Niles "Nat" Turner, Christopher "Sunni Ali Ber" A. Batts and all other African American boys and men in grave danger today. With acknowledgment to my daughters Joyce, Marsha, Renee; and granddaughter Lisa.

This message is in great honor and respect to our Creator and those African ancestors who made my way clear, especially my mother Mary Elizabeth Robinson. It also takes a village to write a book. Therefore, I'd like to thank: Dr. Molefi K. Asante, who responded with resource information and the chapter on "Contemporary Black Scholars"; Professor Luther Jackson, Jr., who guided me on the pathway of journalism; Mrs. Mary Copeland Leftwich for her competent and cheerful assistance with the manuscript; my friend Miss Audrey Russell for volunteering to sacrifice her summer afternoons to proofread with me; to all my many students, colleagues and friends who have helped me and supported my efforts to bring to light the plight of African Americans, mainly because of the war against African American men and youths.

Contents

Updated Introduction

In the first edition of *In Fear of African American Men: The Four Fears of White Men*, the focus was black men's strength, intelligence, sexuality and anger. Purdue University professors David Rollock and Scott Vrana, developed a scientific experiment wiring white male subjects. Reported in the *Journal of Psychophysiology*, July 1998, "Physiological response to a minimal social encounter: Effects of gender, ethnicity, and social context." The study disclosed that when an African American man walked into a room of wired white men, the white men's hearts jumped ten beats a minute. Why did the mere sight of black men produce such a profound reaction in the white men? Rollock and Vrana speculated the reaction could have been unfamiliarity with black men, stereotyping and media portraying them as burly and violent. Conversely, when white men walked into a room of wired black men the reaction was only about 2%. The Perdue study was aborted, but the evidence helps to establish the validity of at least two of the "Four Fears"—"Strength" and "Anger."

IMAGES CREATED TO DEHUMANIZE, DEMEAN, DEGRADE

The first edition documented Hollywood's role in dehumanizing, demeaning and degrading African American males since the 1900's. Sadly, at this time, some black Hollywood screenwriters, producers and actors follow Hollywood's legacy in films stereotyping black males as gangsters and buffoons. Films and videos are major influences on black youths' murdering and maming each other. Some black men's roles in films by whites have improved, but often they are still one-dimensional characters: cop, detective, doctor, lawyer, athlete or sidekick. This year, Hollywood attempted to repair its racist history.

But Hollywood held on to its skullduggery in awarding both Oscars. In "Training Day," Denzel Washington, who played outstanding roles in

"Malcolm X," and "Hurricane," portrayed a vicious, rogue cop. In "Monster's Ball," Halle Berry, who has played decent roles, was cast as an underclass woman whose troubled life was an excuse to succumb to animalistic sex scenes with a white racist, her executed husband's former jailer.

IMAGES OF CONTEMPORARY BLACK MEN

This year *Newsweek Magazine* put three black CEO's of major U.S. corporations on its cover implying that now black men can make it to the highest levels. In the same issue black reporter Ellis Coss offers "New Rules For Black Men"... "Don't be too proud to ask for help, don't complain; play the race card at your own peril; don't expect competence and hard work alone to get you recognition; know the structure is a 'social body' that rewards those fully engaged in the game!" What Coss failed to say is that his rules are for black men who have mastered the basics; significant numbers can't get to that place. In other words, according to Coss' thesis, give up being a conscious African American man; just join white culture if you want to succeed.

Still, the prevailing image of black males is by way of television news showing brothers as murderers, rapists, and drug dealers; otherwise it's athletes, entertainers, and actors. The World Trade Center bombers traveled around the U.S. unchallenged and lived wherever they chose. They enrolled in flight school but did not practice landing a plane. Cops and authorities have implanted in their brains that they must profile and control African American men. Therefore, white skinned men are not profiled; they can murder and bomb with alacrity. For example, the mass murders in Oklahoma, California, Columbine and other schools. Since Nat Turner's insurrection no black man has slaughtered whites, yet black men are still paying for that event.

THE BELL CURVE, SAME OLD BULL CURVE

The first edition documented generations of relentless efforts by scientific racists tried to prove African American's innate inferiority. *The African Presence in Early Asia*, Runoko Rashidi (Ed) & Ivan Van

Setrtima, Transaction Publishers, December 1987, covers more than 500,000 years of the first Homo erectus migrations out of Africa. Association for the Advancement of Science, *Science*, Vol. 271, Mar. 9, 1966, K.K. Kidd, Yale Department of Genetics, research on DNA Global Patterns reported the best known genetic evidence used to support the African origin of mankind has come from studies of DNA traced back through maternal lineage to a single ancestor that existed in Africa between 100,000 and 300,000 years ago. Furthermore, in the research it became evident that West Africans have the highest DNA (haplotype) markers demonstrated in a STRP allele (bp) chart meaning West Africans among non African populations are the physiologically strongest humans in the world. The Yale researchers concluded sub-Saharan African populations...constitute some of the strongest evidence to date...Extolling the idea of superiority comes from those who are committed to scientific racism as a means to dominate and control.

ATROCITIES

For over fifteen years University of Pennsylvania Professor Dr. Albert M. Kligman conducted experiments on black male prisoners in Holmesburg Prison, Philadelphia, Pennsylvania. Kligman introduced infectious diseases, radioactive isotopes, dioxin, and psychotropic drugs without their knowledge; they were maimed and seriously injured. *Acres of Skin: Human Experiments at Holmesburg Prison: A True Story of Abuse and Exploitation in the Name of Medical Science*, Allen M. Hornblum. "Ninety percent of the 300 victims were Black men awaiting trial, not able to make bail; they may have been innocent. The experiments allegedly led to the discovery of the billion-dollar drug "Retin-A."

Brian Wronge, a prisoner, reported in the first edition how he claimed he was involuntarily implanted with a paramagnetic chip.A recent article in "Vanity Fair Magazine" by Paul Someson said that British Professor Keven Warwick actually had a "silicon-based transponder surgically inserted in his forearm. Benefits of being "chipped" are passing toll booths, the paralyzed move limbs, eliminating passwords and implanting devises in kidnap prone executives.

Wronge suffered pain, terrorism, and ridicule from the experiment. Warwick's tests, may not be directly related, nevertheless, prisoners, are often used against their will for science, and implemented for others benefit.

INJUSTICES AND IMPRISONMENTS

Six million are incarcerated in the U. S. *Stolen Lives-killed by law enforcement,* 1999, presents over 2,000 cases of killings by law enforcement between 1990 and 1999 in the stepped up "WAR ON DRUGS" by President Clinton. They used excessive force: brutality, shooting, hog-tying, choke hold, "suicide by cop," police dogs, asphyxiation,etc. The National Center on Addiction reported in 1998 that 1.4 million of the two million inmates are incarcerated for drugs, alcohol or substance abuse. NOT FELONIES. Those inmates have 2.4 MILLION CHILDREN LIVING WITHOUT A PARENT. *The Haverford Alumni Magazine* "Friendly Fire," Spring 2000, tells how the war is waged with Nazi storm trooper methods on minorities. Before dawn, homes are broken into by officers in masks with assault weapons and devices that stun and disorient the occupants. Children are routed from their beds by masked men and held at gunpoint.

Legalizing drugs, is a possible solution, The strongest objections come from police and other agencies that are the beneficiaries of the "WAR ON DRUGS." Costs jumped from $683 million in 1975 to $17.7 billion in 1999. Eric C. Sterling, President of the "Criminal Justice Policy Foundation" says the current policy makes violence the only means of doing business in narcotics. Drug dealers can't hire police for protection; the drug trade can only be curtailed if it is regulated and taken away from criminal cartels. Only now in 2002 are some state governments and congress making attempts to change the unfair mandatory drug sentencing laws.

Introduction

Racism, the tool of white supremacy, is rooted in white men's Four Fears of African American men: fear of their strength, intelligence, sexuality and anger. The fears are individual, interrelated, and unitary; they are the underlying, unspoken reasons for attitudes, beliefs and actions that have shaped the destinies and lives of black men, such as the common accusation, "A Black Man Did It." This book serves to develop a deeper and multi-faceted understanding of the causes and solutions to problems that arise as a result of the Four Fears. More important, however, is the earnest hope that the book will motivate people to organize to establish rules of conduct for dealing with the system and each other to serve as a unified policy to take action for survival.

It is common to look at the Four Fears separately; however, looking at them as an operating unit presents an entirely different picture. For example, any one of the fears can be intimidating be it strength, intelligence, sexuality or anger, but operating as a unit they overwhelm the adversaries of black men because they tend to provoke powerful emotional and psychological reactions, particularly in white men. In addition, the Four Fears represent awesome power potential because of the history of African peoples' victories over adversity and their ability to endure horrific conditions and arise victorious. The Four

Fears were personified in white men's perceptions of such men as Marcus Garvey, W.E.B. DuBois, Paul Robeson, Adam Clayton Powell, Malcolm X and everyday African American men who never get a chance to excel.

The cases and histories in this book prove that the individual fears elicit angst in whites. Intelligent African American men represent a threat because they have the potential to wrest control from white men in power. Beyond a doubt African and African American men have exhibited superior intelligence from time immemorial until historical circumstances intervened. Indeed, extreme efforts were made to change history and obliterate knowledge of African and African American women's and men's intellect and accomplishments across the realm of modern civilization.

Physical and mental strength are issues of historic consequences in the Four Fears of white men. Physical strength, while admired in sports, is also used as a weapon against black men to depict them as strong but dim-witted. Furthermore, the mental ability of black men throughout the years, in spite of adversity, is viewed as menacing when they are courageous, inventive, knowledgeable, and committed to struggle against tyranny. These elements are vital considerations in the numerous actions to control and destabilize black men.

Fear of African American men's and boys' anger is an outgrowth of white guilt. It is readily understandable given the history of atrocities against African Americans. If they were not angry, they would be mentally deficient. However, more needs to be publicized and acted on to explicate the genesis of this fear of retaliation because fear of retaliation is often used as an excuse to institute preemptive acts against black men.

Perhaps the most threatening of the Four Fears is the fear of African and African American men's sexuality. It is recorded in earliest written documents, across continents, through the ages, up until the present time. Fear of black men's sexuality is integral to the political and economic racism that is dedicated to preventing African American men from assuming their rightful place in society. A few are allowed to get through the system to the top to act as carrots, raise false hopes, or act as gatekeepers. Others are "go along to get along" examples for others. On the other hand, those who take principled stands pay dearly for their audacity and courage. Many times they are also shunned by their black brothers and sisters.

Since 1700, black men have been disproportionately incarcerated throughout the U.S. The Four Fears are directly related to the "lock 'em up and throw away the key," or the latest "three strikes and you're in prison for life" because these measures are indirect ways to eliminate those who have the potential for revolt. Today the U.S. has the audacity to proclaim that it is a democracy and leader of the free world, blithely ignoring the fact that the U.S. has the highest penal imprisonment rate in the world. White supremacy, primarily, causes African American men to constitute 49 percent of the prison population, while less than 6 percent of the U.S. population.

A significant finding is that it did not matter too much what the status of the black man was: if he were a hard core criminal or a moral, productive, erudite man committed to gaining freedom and a decent life for his race, he could be hounded and brought down like a common criminal. Whether he possessed one or all four of the Four Fears made little difference.

This book has many purposes. It creates fresh fields of knowledge for study and action and enlarges upon previous information. It raises levels of awareness and motivates people to reconsider the reasons behind the attacks on black men. It will also serve the education, business, and legal communities; courts and police actions; any contacts between African American men and other people, particularly white men.

It also raises questions such as: How do the Four Fears affect situations in which black and white men interface as grounds for research, analysis and recognition as contributing factors to the scourge heaped upon African American men? How does the black man see the white man with whom he interfaces? How does it affect the black man's psyche? What fears and stereotypes are black men wrestling with? Do the hidden fears hinder them and cause them to present less secure, less confident composures? What role do the Four

Fears play in the black male and black female relations? For example, are the Four Fears of white men reasons for their preference in hiring black women? It creates a lot of animus amongst black males and females. Or, when a black man is turned down for a job he is clearly qualified for because he is a threat to a white male employer, does this diminish his esteem in his own eyes, his mate's and his family's?

How does the fall out from the Four Fears influence the rest of society? It makes matters more ominous for African Americans because many poor whites buy the hype, thrive on white supremacy and blame blacks for the financial and social ills of the country. A large number of whites are arming themselves and preparing to be vigilantes for these reasons.

What has been done to black men is a sin. How does a Judeo-Christian country justify this truth? Can America ignore what has been done to black men by Judeo-Christians? How can the U.S. survive with the wrongs that threaten the survival of thirty million people?

There are other important issues too. There's a need to dissect and counter the role of the Four Fears in the racist and greedy manipulation of the economy that has produced deep-rooted self hatred in a percentage of deprived black youth.

There are other dangers too facing African Americans. One of the worst outgrowths of exposing racism is the penchant of some black people to use it as an excuse to commit crimes. Using racism as an excuse for wrong behavior weakens the moral fiber and integrity of the black community. Therefore, it is difficult to enforce sanctions and ostracism of black criminals and con artists who feed off their brothers and sisters. It also encourages the criminal justice system to be capricious in meting out justice, i.e. if it's black on black crime a light sentence is meted out, black life is cheap, but if it is black on white, the book is thrown at the accused. How can these issues become part of an agenda for change?

There are intra race dangers too. There is danger in resting on the knowledge in this book and not using it to struggle to change conditions. There is danger in more black mothers making excuses for black sons' misdeeds due to racism. Also, danger in over-protecting black boys for fear of the white man, thereby thwarting their maturation and thus helping to produce angry teens and men. Danger in black opportunists using knowledge of the Four Fears to dupe other blacks and intimidate whites into granting them money and privileges. Danger in ignoring the impact of the Four Fears and continuing to worship false values and acquiring materialism at the expense of human, family values, and cultural cohesion.

This book is not to engender more finger pointing, because it is a well founded fact that white supremacy is the primary issue that adversely affects African Americans. Understanding, prioritizing concerns and taking consistent action are the critical considerations at this time. The multitude of black individuals and groups concerned with the plight of black males and looking for solutions can use this book to initiate various approaches to the critical issues discussed. Once the underlying causes for the reasons African American men and boys are treated like pariahs in this society are fully understood and confronted, steps toward overcoming the serious individual life and race threatening attitudes and practices can be implemented.

OVERCOMING OBSTACLES

1
Images Created To
Dehumanize, Demean, Degrade

The Bible story of Noah in Genesis (from the very start) has been used to create disparaging images of black men. Supremacists and racists have gone so far as to interpret accounts of Noah's son Ham as a law breaker and subject to sub-human behavior. The story of Noah says Ham's descendants were cursed with black skin for this act. However, *Race: The History of an Idea*, states nothing is written in Genesis about Ham being punished. Nor, Canaan's descendants (Ethiopians) sentenced forever to be the servants of the world, another allegation. "This *idea* is not found until the oral traditions of the Jews were collected in Babylonian Talmud from the second to the sixth Century, A.D."[1] It's also reported that God forbade sexual relations on Noah's Ark, but Ham disobeyed this command. Still another legend claims Ham was cursed with black skin because he castrated his father to prevent a rival heir. Versions of Ham's alleged fall from grace vary, but the theme is the same, black men have committed reprehensible acts since the Garden of Eden. (Some also say the snake who tempted Adam in the Garden was a black woman.) Other interpretations charge Ham had forbidden sex on the Ark , with the animals. Additional punishment reported to be in the Talmud depicts all of Ham's descendants being led into captivity with their buttocks uncovered as a mark of degradation. (This theme is repeated in racist literature, art and artifacts. In addition, for years white police have a reputation for baring black men's buttocks to dehumanize them: cases like the notorious, bigot and bully, police chief, Frank Rizzo stripping Black Panthers naked in the streets of Philadelphia in the 1970s. As late as August of 1997, in Brooklyn, New York, cops made a black male prisoner walk around the police station house with his pants around his ankles before sodomizing him with a bathroom plunger, seriously rupturing his internal organs and then ramming the plunger in his mouth, breaking out his front teeth.)

Another misinterpretation of the Bible used as a slur against black people is "Can an Ethiopian change his skin or a leopard his spots?" (Jer. 13:23). The question was not meant to connote that black skin was a negative branding by God.

These statements taken from the Bible and Talmud have been used against Africans and African Americans for over 5,000 years. It is crystal clear that the Four Fears of African American men have been, in fact, handed down in print, music, and art as God's curse of black people.

Using words allegedly handed down from God, stereotyping and making scapegoats are very effective in creating derogatory images. Images are more impressive than words because they elicit conditioned responses without thinking. Long-standing beliefs and traditions buttressed by public policies, literature, laws and mass media, specifically film, television, radio and video, are indelible marks. They are difficult to deprogram when intentional historical lies about religion, history and mentality are proclaimed by powerful sources. For instance, in order to obliterate the greatness of traditional Africa before the invasions of the Arabs, Asians and others, the lies about God's relationship with Africans and the Four Fears of white men played important roles in justifying invasions and the plundering of African resources.

The Destruction of Black Civilization says the invaders waged centuries-long battles against Africans. Chancellor Williams writes, "I... still wonder how any people, weakened by perpetual hunger and disease, could possibly carry on wars of resistance to the white invaders for over 5,000 years. This they did and this their descendants must know and remember with pride."[2]

As sub-Saharan Africa became isolated from Northern Africa and interaction along trade routes, African cultures were less materially and technologically oriented; they focused on traditional values and rituals. Therefore, they were easy prey for the European invaders who had developed superior military power. Using their technological advances and religion it became "the white man's burden" to civilize "the savage." Together they joined forces to conquer and enslave. Furthermore, internecine conflicts among Africans, avarice and the common practice of taking and selling slaves created the worse holocaust of modern times. Due to the untold millions of Africans who were uprooted and sold into slavery, African people were set back centuries. At the same time, many of their descendants are still struggling to make and keep gains. Slavery built this country for over two hundred years without pay and approximately two hundred years later African Americans are still working for less pay.

Immediately upon declaration of the truce between the North and South, a renewed anti black movement started during Reconstruction and it continues on various levels despite the significant and remarkable gains made by African Americans. An inept, racist, white supremacist doctor, Thomas Dixon, led the anti emancipation struggle using the Bible to support his diatribes. *The Clansman* and *The Leopard's Spots*, using biblical defamation, said blacks could not change their ignorant, lustful, savage ways. "The Negro was not a citizen and an equal, not even a child as yet unprepared. He was a semi-savage descendant of an old and degenerate animal race."[3] Herein is the establishment of images of black people in words in popular literature at the start of their struggle to overcome the holocaust of slavery. In slavery they were forbidden education or reading books. Valiantly trying to make it on their own with only the memories of skilled labor and farming handed down from their African ancestors, they toiled around the clock, nursed, fed, built and farmed for their slave masters. But the derogation by media was more effective than a recitation of the vicissitudes of slavery. The black man was nothing more than "…a thick-lipped, flat-nosed, spindle-shanked Negro, exuding his nauseating animal odor," said Dixon.[4]

The Clansman was mass marketed to vilify and lie about black men. Dixon's sensationalism was guaranteed to induce emotional reaction; he depicted black men as "brutes" and "lechers" bent on raping and ravaging white women. This theme became the propaganda for the lynching and burning at the stake of over four thousand black men. An infamous example of this racist social behavior is the Rosewood Florida case, where an entire black community was destroyed on the basis of a rumor that a black man assaulted a white woman. This case is not an isolated incident.

A torrent of racist books and articles was published to defile African Americans after the Civil War. Books pretending to have the last word of science concerning the importance of race and the nature of Negroes multiplied. Charles Carroll's *The Negro a Beast*, or William P. Calhoun's *The Caucasian and the Negro in the United States* (1902); William B. Smith's *The Color Line: A Brief on Behalf of the Unborn* (1905); and Robert W. Shufeldt's *The Negro, A Menace to American Civilization* (1907) were books passionately devoted to the theme of Negro inferiority."[5] Magazines, articles and pamphlets were also mass produced on this subject. Thomas Nelson Page wrote, "The negroes *as a race* have never exhibited any capacity to advance, that as a race they are inferior, and the fact that there were a few Negro doctors and lawyers proved nothing but that they had white blood in their veins."[6]

Words defaming African Americans were put with film to establish negative images in the most effective way. Building on the racism of the literature of Dixon, filmmaker D. W. Griffith made Dixon's *The Clansman* into the infamous film *Birth of a Nation*. It was immediately declared "the greatest motion picture." Therein the motion picture industry gave birth to the demonization of African Americans on film, particularly black men. *Birth of a Nation* portrayed black men as wild people foraging about to rape white women, kill or steal from whites.

In the years after Emancipation a primary motivation for demonizing black men was the fear of black economic development—intelligence fear. Many of the burnings and lynchings were to stop black people from gaining economic independence. This effort has prevailed down through the years in job, housing and education discrimination.

Dixon's book *The Clansman* was the handbook for the Ku Klux Kian and Griffith's movie was used to solicit membership in the Klan. Thus, it is clear that the demonization of black men is rooted in literature and film and contributed to Klan murders and intimidations which prevented African American men from gaining an economic foothold after slavery. The early planned discrimination is the historic basis, carried on down through the years by nefarious methods, for the low levels of black economic development today. It takes decades of continued economic viability to succeed in business. Destructive images have played one of the most important roles in holding back progress.

Griffith, the Klan and Hollywood latched on to the pre Civil War minstrel stage show tradition. It sustained the negation of the humanity of African Americans to support the prevalence of political and economic slavery. The talented, famous Bert Williams, a black minstrel, had to blacken his light skin, slouch and speak in dialect in the early twentieth century. (Unfortunately, today, the phenomenon of identifying with the oppressor, has some black actors and actresses portraying Sambo, Aunt Jemima and Rastus images to get work on television, stage and in motion pictures.)

The "bad nigger" brute image in *Birth of a Nation* was preceded in 1894 in Thomas Edison's first film *The Pickaninnies Doing a Dance*. He took pains to deride innocent black children in his first film. However, Edison apparently did not credit African American, Lewis Latimer, who invented the carbon filament for the electric bulb, in a well-known medium.

In 1907, the film *Dancing Nig* started the genre of black men as dancing clowns and fools on the silver screen. Black men were routinely cast as dishonest, sly, lazy, watermelon-loving and bug-eyed, and were often chicken thieves.

To show the early and continued connection between the U.S. Congress and Hollywood, when Jack Johnson, the great black fighter, beat the "great white hope," Jim Jefferies, Congress went so far as to pass a law that prevented any interstate showing of prize fights. This law prevented people across the United States from viewing the ignominy of a black man beating a white man. Congress, the highest law making body in the United States, consistently makes laws and passes resolutions that aid and abet the demonization of African American men.

In the 1940s and 50s a few films started to cast black men as normal humans; however, they were one dimensional eunuchs. Their relationships were restricted to interacting with white main characters. The black character's personal relationships, ambitions, and hopes were ignored. One example is black actor Dooley Wilson, the famous Sam the piano player in *Casablanca,* the 1942 Humphrey Bogart movie. Much was known about the character Bogart played, but nothing about Sam. The line "Play it again, Sam" is legend, but Sam is not. There is more universal memory of bug-eyed, stupid acting Mantan Moreland, famous for crying "feet don't fail me now," as he fled wild-eyed and terrified from imagined ghosts and unexplained activities.

In the years of Hollywood censorship before the Sodom and Gomorra on film and video of today, censorship boards scrupulously critiqued films with black actors to insure the basic Four Fears of white men were not aroused. When Hollywood was caught between local film censors who did not want any interracial activity, or the objections of the NAACP to stereotyped black characters, movie studios simply wrote or edited them out of the script or the film. Many black actors were thrown out of work. Hattie McDaniel, famous for her Academy Award winning role as Mammy in *Gone With the Wind,* said she had the choice of either playing Mammy or being one.

Gradually, the NAACP succeeded in pressuring Hollywood to open jobs, resulting in black actors as cops, extras, and workers. However, this apparent portend of dignified roles was a false foreshadowing. New black caricatures such as "Superfly" and "Superspade" erupted in black exploitation films. *From Sambo to Superspade* points out that "although he was as defamatory and inhuman as Sambo had been, Superspade was at least emotionally more satisfying to most black moviegoers."7 Superspade types were ghetto hero types and African Americans turned out in droves to see black men play daring roles, being killers and being killed just as the white gangsters and movie cop heroes they had idolized before.

The black exploitation and Superspade movies rescued Hollywood from certain death from the growing success of television. Since then, African Americans, mainly youths, have been the loyal, financial base of the Hollywood motion picture business. Brainwashed, brain dead, cultureless blacks support the dehumanizing images of themselves as murderers, pimps, and hired killers. Black moviegoers spend millions to venerate sex, gold, cars, clothes, sneakers, revenge for power and perceived disrespect in which worthwhile lessons are lost on the majority. Modern movies overflow with images of black men such as Dixon's "brutes": disrespectful, swaggering, emotional, angry, and homicidal. They cause their own demise as they copy and use the means gleaned from films to destroy each other. These are the 1990's version of black male images created in *Birth of a Nation*. The imitators assume the behavior of the former oppressors. It is not uncommon. The glorious stories of African American history with all of its heroes, heroines, and liberators are purposely prevented from being filmed and distributed. They lie fallow as destructive images triumph.

Other negative images proliferated in other venues after the Civil War for the same reasons as in literature and film. A deluge of negative images of African Americans was initiated by product advertisers, and they co-conspired with the movie and book authors to malign black citizens. Numerous products carried grinning visages of "darkies," cooking, eating watermelon, with words in dialect in drawings and pictures. The negative images were presented in every imaginable category; the extent is beyond belief. The biblical myths of being banished for disobedience to God were prevalent. Black men with bared buttocks and black men and boys sitting on the toilet or potty were also common. Eating watermelon and stealing chickens were the most popular themes in toys, silverware, china. Souvenirs were extremely popular in the form of post cards, ceramics, trinkets of all sorts. No aspect of black life was spared.

Some reports say that African American images were used on food product ads because they were looked upon as good cooks and domestic workers. However, if that were true, why were they castigated and made to look like fools? Here again, stupid looking, slovenly, savage visages were utilized to sell products by manufacturers and advertisers. A late 1880s tobacco can had a so-called African pictured with wild woolly hair and rings in his nose. The tobacco was called "Nigger Hair." Still in use in the 1950s, the NAACP registered a protest; the company responded by renaming it "Bigger Hair" instead of "Nigger Hair," and retained the picture.

Aunt Jemima has gone through many changes, even foregoing her head rag and lightening her skin. Rastus, her boyfriend, on early boxes of Cream of Wheat was eventually eliminated. Neither African American women nor children were spared from the vicious movement. Together with film, the images have had a stronger influence than racist words in instigating and perpetuating racism.

Incorrectly called "black Memorabilia," these negative artifacts should be called "White Racist Memorabilia" because there are some outstanding positive portrayals of African Americans in print, art and artifacts which should not be confused with the negative ones. The black images from that era are big business with large numbers of black and white collectors, but the millionaire collectors are predominantly white. Here also as in the case of film, television, print and stage plays, some blacks have joined the oppressor in making and selling negative images of themselves and their ancestors. These behaviors are what Amos N. Wilson names "inculcating the beast."[8] Other races guard their racial identity and have their cultural cement intact. They zealously resist disparaging themselves, but the Americans, Japanese, French, Germans, English, South Africans and others have made millions demonizing the images of African Americans, especially black men.

2
Images of Contemporary African American Men

O. J. Simpson's murder case was mega fodder for the mass media campaign to deprecate African American males by making prominent black men scapegoats for popularized social ills. Recent media reporting and imagery personifies prominent black men as brutes. Subsequently, these men are used as examples for new laws, books, movies, television talk shows, conferences and college courses. First, let's be clear. Some of these prominent black men, on the whole, are media created leaders. They are not African American men with demonstrated commitment and sacrifice in the struggle to liberate and educate African Americans to be self determining economically, culturally and socially. On the other hand, a few are. The point is that negative portrayals of prominent black men, slanders black men in general.

"A Black Man Did It"—the practice of placing a black man's face on crime—reached a frenzy in the O.J. Simpson double murder case. It comes from the tradition since enslavement of falsely accusing black men of crimes. In the past, black men were also depicted as lazy with criminal tendencies and irrational behavior—menaces to society. The media and portions of literature diligently perpetuated the "strong back, weak mind" stereotype of the black athlete, but those stereotypes have been refuted, Lately, famous black men in the news are projected as examples of the customary belief that "A Black Man Did It" if a crime is committed.

Since 1994, O.J. Simpson has been the symbol for spousal abuse. Simpson betrayed his media-image as the black hero football star who escaped the ghetto and embraced the white world. But now he is the poster man for spousal abuse. It's certainly commendable that some battered women took action and changed their personal situations as a result of the hype, but the media's use of Simpson's case to deface black men for social causes is one of the worst examples in history of the designation of "A Black Man Did It."

Simpson joins singer Michael Jackson as a similar poster icon. Jackson was vilified by the press as a symbol for child sexual abuse. However, the epidemic of cases against white priests charged with sexual molestation of boys, fornication and homosexuality are not sensationalized by tabloid news reporting.

Boxing champion Mike Tyson was made the symbol for date rape. His image as the incarnate black rapist was splashed across the globe too. Suddenly date rape was the hot topic for talk shows and magazine articles. Based on the facts of the case, Tyson's stiff jail sentence far outweighed the crime, but it was intended to demean the image of a prominent black man. (It also encouraged efforts to destroy his manager, Don King, because he makes money the way white managers did in the past—off black boxers.)

Ben Chavis, former NAACP head, who had a record for sacrifice and struggle in the Civil Rights movement, was made a symbol for sex discrimination and harassment. However, the attacks on him were not because Chavis allegedly discriminated against a woman, it was more likely because he invited Louis Farrakhan of the Nation of Islam to a conference. Nobody cared about the NAACP's peccadilloes and offenses before that alliance. The idea of the NAACP and the NOI joining forces is a serious economic and political threat and Chavis' image had to be defaced.

Clarence Thomas was the start of the sexual harassment symbol. Although he is a travesty to the memory, record and legacy of the

Honorable Supreme Court Justice Thurgood Marshall whom Thomas succeeded, to some white media and conservatives he is a prominent black man. Telecasts of Thomas' Supreme Court nomination hearings with charges alleged against him by Anita Hill, a former black employee, shocked and titillated viewers. His hearings were the forerunner of the Simpson media thrill show. Hill was allegedly egged on by white feminists, and Thomas, the Republican's puppet, took advantage of the racial guilt of the white Democrat male senators and accused them of a "high tech lynching." They caved in and put this menace to black people on the bench; and when the dust settled, the sensationalism resulted in the imagery of a black man for new legislation.

Black and white men who are guilty of sexual harassment and abuse should be dealt with. However, there is no comparable set of prominent white men exposed to the same degree as symbols, stereotypes and bellwethers of rape, abuse and anti-feminism. Black men are held to higher standards than white men in all cases and kept under closer scrutiny by the media, the police, the courts, officials in government and business. The saddest fact is that many black people believe "A Black Man Did It" because of the media.

Add to the list, Ron Brown, deceased former Secretary of Commerce; Mike Espy, former Secretary of Agriculture; Dr. Henry Foster, trashed candidate for Surgeon General; Louis Farrakhan; Marion Berry, whom the government spent millions to catch smoking dope merely because he was a prominent black man. By contrast, Ollie North, former White House aide, traded guns and drugs, endangering lives and destabilizing countries, and merely got a slap on the wrist.

The consistent use of black men to personify crime and misconduct is grossly unfair. Not only is it harmful to them, it affects ethics and morality among African Americans. This is a critical issue in the black community. Many people are motivated to defend criminals and to justify criminal acts due to the history of atrocities against black men.

Fortunately, more African Americans recognize the pattern and know the history of "A Black Man Did It." Exposure of the symbols and stereotypes in white mass media should create and organize a mass movement to target advertisers with selective patronage, using African Americans' considerable middle class economic power, including the huge funds generated in black churches. It could be an effective tool against the practice of saying "A Black Man Did It," prominent or not.

3
The Bell Curve, Same Old Bull Curve

The underlying motivation for scientific racism is white men's fears of African American men. Black people in general are attacked, but African American men are the primary target of degradation and dehumanization, thereby laying grounds for inhumane treatment. Periodically, since the early 1880s pseudo scientific reports have been publicized claiming "proof" that Africans and African Americans are inferior to whites. *The Bell Curve*[1] is an example of so-called scientific evidence that African Americans are inherently inferior. Richard Herrnstein and Charles Murray resurrect earlier theories that African Americans have lower IQ's because of genetic factors. In the past other specious arguments attempting to establish black inferiority have been proposed such as environmental conditions and isolation from whites.

Criminality and inferiority have been linked in depictions of black men, as stated previously. Since black men continue to be the main objects of scorn, unless otherwise stated, racial inferiority claims are focused on them and black boys. However, long before the influence of mass media black men were targets. Since 1790, African American men have been unjustly imprisoned. Innumerable vicious labels, accusations and laws to control and eliminate African Americans have been promulgated. Today, Herrnstein's and Murray's findings support movements in the U.S. to deprive, humiliate, incarcerate, and attempt to destroy black men. Selling 400,000 copies of the book right off the press, *The Bell Curve* is a handbook for the enactment of laws and public policy dedicated to making African Americans scapegoats for societal failures in the U.S. Some of the recommendations justify removal of unproductive blacks from public view. Herrnstein and Murray write, "Economic growth passes them by...technology is not a partner in their lives. Furthermore...their presence hovers over the town...and countryside...creating fear and resentment in the rest of society that is seldom openly expressed but festers nonetheless."[2] Obviously the imagery is African American men and youths.

The Bell Curve was craftily released in time to impact the 1994 national elections that swept the Republicans into office. Within weeks of publication, the president of Rutgers University was telling his faculty that they had to recognize the inherent inferiority of African American students. The book also attempts to certify attacks on school desegregation as well as educational and training opportunities for disadvantaged African Americans. Herrnstein and Murray also claim that black children have low cognitive skills because of absent fathers.

The authors express disdain for programs to bring African Americans parity with the majority. "They (programs) propose solutions founded in better education, or more and better jobs or special social interventions...[But] to try to come to grips with the nation's problems without understanding the role of intelligence...is to grope with symptoms instead of causes to stumble into supposed remedies that have no chance of working."[3] By reviving the intelligence factor, Herrnstein and Murray reinforce linkages with earlier scientific racists. They periodically publish new attacks on African and African American intelligence.

Francis Galton, a descendent of Charles Darwin, coined the term eugenics, selective breeding to create superior qualities of race. It is charged, however, that his objective was to create a master white race and to prove that whites were inherently superior to blacks. Galton said, "The average intellectual standard of the Negro race...is some two grades below [whites]."[4] However, racial designations and derision came about around the time of European expansion and imperialism. Sharon Begley writing in Newsweek, said racial division was instituted during the Age of Exploration. "Before the Europeans took to the seas, there was little perception of races."[5] In 1758, a Swedish taxonomist, Carolus Linnaeus, best known for his system of classifying living things declared that "Africans were indolent and negligent, and Europeans were inventive and gentle."[6] Linnaeus was first to scientifically categorize the people of the world. He names four races, but the only negative comparison was to Africans.

In this era, Herrnstein and Murray attempt to substantiate black I.Q. deficiency using crime and violence statistics in the place of the "indolent and negligent." The say I.Q. scores are significant markers in the commission of crimes—black and white. However, since the I.Q. levels of blacks are lower than whites, Herrnstein and Murray deduce that black crime is also caused by genetic reasons. According to reliable sources, many young, incarcerated black males do have low reading and writing skills. However, this does not necessarily support the low I.Q. theory. Unfortunately, prison is the first place most black male prisoners can obtain a decent education. Many not only obtain their GED, some also earn higher degrees. Regrettably, in this period of mean spiritedness toward criminals, there are moves afoot to cut off these avenues of education. Is this evidence of the gentle character ascribed to Europeans?

Begley says, "Leave aside the racist undertones (not to mention the oddity of ascribing gentleness to the group that perpetrated the Crusades and the Inquisition)… More worrisome is the notion and the specifics of race predate genetics, evolutionary biology and the science of human origins. With the revolutions in those fields, how is it that the 18th century scheme of race retains its powerful hold?"[7] Begley concludes, "We must ask science, also, why it is that we are so intent on sorting humanity into so few groups—us and others—in the first place?"[8] The answers point to the obvious, the desperate need to maintain white supremacy. More recent studies point to the absurdity of attempting to classify races as superior and inferior.

Harvard biologist Richard Lewontian analyzed seventeen genetic markers in 168 populations and determined there is more genetic difference within one race than there is between that race and another.

Scientist Loring Brace says, "Every ethnic group evolved under conditions where intelligence was a requirement for survival. If there are intelligence 'genes,' they must be in all ethnic groups equally: differences in intelligence must be a cultural and social artifact."[9] Since African people are the original people and the longest survivors on earth, based on Brace's findings, and other accredited sources, they cannot be inherently inferior as ascribed by *The Bell Curve*. "Its authors have become celebrities among fascists, skinheads and the scientific posse… Herrnstein and Murray say what you always believed about black folk is not really racism, its science," states Dr. Anthony Monteiro.[10] Murray says he does not promote racial strife, but he admitted on television that he burned a cross on the lawn of a black family when he was a student. And, Herrnstein (deceased) was a pillar in the scientific racism movement during his life. "Going further they argued that since poverty, crime and low IQ test scores are biologically produced, the poor should be subjected to forced sterilization, concentration camps, starvation, forced labor at below minimum wages and imprisonment for children," according to Dr. Monteiro.[11] He goes on to say that the book "says absolutely nothing new. Unless one considers new the claim that black men's alleged abnormally large penises are a sign of their supposed intellectual inferiority."[12]

Reasons behind labeling Africans and African Americans in the Era of Exploration are clarified by Cheikh Anta Diop in his discussion of "Birth of the Negro Myth" (inherited inferiority) in *The African Origin of Civilization*. Africans had a preeminent history dating back many thousands of years. Over time Africans from the region of the Nile River penetrated deep into the interior of the continent and established centers of civilization. Eventually they became cut off from access routes to the Mediterranean due to shifting atmospheric conditions. Subsequently, that contingent was completely isolated when Egypt lost its independence due to invasions by conquering armies.

Over the years they had become oriented toward concentrating upon their social, political and moral organization. Moreover, the scientific, agricultural and construction expertise developed along the Nile were not needed in the living conditions in the interior, according to Diop.[13] As previously stated, Africans' economic resources were not dependent upon perpetual technological inventiveness. Therefore, they gradually became indifferent to material progress.

"It was under these new conditions that the encounter with Europe took place," notes Diop.[14] European traders set up posts on the West Coast of Africa. They found African political and social organization in order, and contrary to white traders and missionaries, African kings were not despotic rulers. Diop says, "The social and moral order was on the same level of perfection."[15] However, Africa became vulnerable and easy prey because of the European's superior technology, weapons, and because of internal strife among various tribes.

Eventually, the economic progress of Europe grew as their military might increased and their relations with Africans progressed from trading to annexation and pacification. "Such a reversal of roles, the result of new technical relations, brought with it master-slave relationships between whites and blacks..."[16] Diop also writes that the Europeans, by virtue of their technical superiority, started to look down on the black world and stooped to stealing their riches. "The record and the memory of 'Negro Egypt' (or Ethiopia) that civilized the world had been blurred by ignorance of the antique tradition hidden in libraries or buried under ruins."[17] Ignorance, indifference, prejudice, combined with motivation to exploit "...predisposed the mind of the European to distort the moral personality of the black and his intellectual aptitudes."[18]

> Henceforth, "Negro" became a synonym for a primitive being, "inferior," endowed with a pre-logical mentality. As the human being is always eager to justify his conduct, [the enslavers] went even further. The desire to legitimize colonization and the slave trade—in

23

other words, the social condition of the Negro in the modern world—engendered an entire literature to describe the so-called inferior traits of the black. The mind of several generations of Europeans would thus be gradually indoctrinated, Western opinion would crystallize and instinctively accept as revealed truth the equation: Negro=inferior humanity....They invoked "the civilizing mission"...from then on capitalism had clear sailing to practice the most ferocious exploitation under the cloak of moral pretexts.[19]

Subsequently, a French racist, Arthur de Gobineau, 1816-1882, an antecedent to Herrnstein and Murray and their like, published *The Inequality of Human Races*.[20] Nowhere in history do you find Africans attacking and dehumanizing Europeans as did de Gobineau.

In 1994, *The Bell Curve* authors perpetuated the myth of black inferiority like their ancestors who used scientific theory to validate their claims of superiority. They are about the business of using the inferiority myth to justify laws that create additional hardships on the most disadvantaged in the society, poor African American men. These are the descendants of slavery who are no longer essential in the age of technology when they are also feared for the righteous and justifiable anger. Thus, for those reasons and others, Africans in America, like Africans in Africa, are the victims of racism and technology again. Herrnstein's and Murray's remedies, outgrowths of the myth of inherited inferiority, will be excuses behind claims that government sponsored programs don't work, that education is impossible, that employment training is a waste, etc. Waiting down the line to consume the desperate and the uneducated African American men and youths is the booming, huge prison industry—modern slave labor camps. Other deprived black men are more prone to be victims of the violent and vicious drug trade, or other hostile actions. In addition, less obvious factors cause African American men to succumb to homelessness and suffer due to lack of access to health care, poor nutrition, dangerous and poorly paid work.

Herrnstein and Murray did not have to reach too deep for their "inherited inferiority" thesis, their authorities come forth every few decades. In the 1950s and 60s, it was the likes of Wesley C. George, Professor Emeritus of Anatomy at The University of North Carolina; Audrey M. Shuey, Psychologist, Randolph Macon College, Lynchburg, Virginia; Frank McGurk, Villanova University, Villanova, Pennsylvania;[21] and historian, Carelton Putman, *Race and Reason* labeled the white Citizen's Councils' handbook.[22] They all aligned with a major spokesman for scientific racism, Henry E. Garrett, former head of the Psychology Department, Columbia University, New York City.[23] He authored articles on inferiority of negroes, i.e. "The Equalitarian Dogma," *Mankind Quarterly*.[24] It has ties to the Pioneer Fund.[25] The Pioneer Fund alleges it is dedicated to race betterment in the United States. This group has been behind eugenics propaganda in films and literature distributed throughout the United States.[26]

Herrnstein and Murray are allied with the Pioneer Fund, founded in 1937, bankrolled by a New England, millionaire merchant. The leadership lauded Nazi Germany's racial science. In 1954, the fund opposed the Brown v. Board of Education of Topeka decision. After the 1964 Civil Rights bill passed, the fund actively opposed programs for the poor including Head Start. It proclaimed that "The academic performance of black students was the result of irreversible genetic deficiencies." Therefore, the programs wasted tax money. During the same period, the Pioneer Fund gave racist scientist, Authur Jensen a one million dollar research grant. In the late 60s Jensen published a thesis on the inherited inferiority of African Americans. Although they did not receive money from the Pioneer Fund for the book, "Herrnstein and Murray use the works of many social scientists connected with the Pioneer Fund for *The Bell Curve*."[27]

Arthur Jensen and collaborator William Shockley, also allegedly financially supported by the Pioneer Fund, have the public reputation of notoriety on the subject of Black inferiority. Herrnstein and Murray cited Jensen as their main source for accusations that African Americans and Africans are intellectually inferior.

The depth and length of the prodigious efforts to debase Africans and African Americans speaks volumes validating the strength, intelligence and superior ability to withstand centuries of abuse and attacks from Caucasians, other races and self-inflicted negative behavior due to circumstances of colonization and caste. Otherwise, why the continual and pernicious, ridiculous machinations over African Americans' intelligence? The attackers act like teased kids having a tantrum shouting over and over "you are! you are! you are!" as if repeating a lie will make it true.

Furthermore, if, as Herrnstein and Murray claim, black students score 15 percent lower on standardized tests (which are culturally and racially biased on the whole), it is the fault of the educational system controlled by whites. Children in black private, free and Muslim schools achieve high scores on standardized tests. The avid white supremacists, and even some of those who have been victims of racism themselves, are devoted to trying to stymie every effort of African Americans to gain equal education opportunities. Nevertheless, the self-admitted failures are resorting to Draconian measures to regain their failing economic system instead of confessing their complicity in fostering racism in the U.S., confess to the reasons behind the failing economy such as imperialistic wars, the Cold War, secret and faulty trade deals with other countries, shipping business and industry overseas for more profit from cheap labor, supporting the illegal drug traffic into the country, and giving away the store in the Savings and Loans thefts by cohorts and cronies. The "Contract for America" was to correct these problems by legislation that in practice would take away from the poor and give to the rich. The move has been tagged Robin Hoods [sic] in reverse. Robbing the Hood is apropos, too. On its face, *The Bell Curve* appears to be a document to undermine socially disadvantaged African Americans, however, there's a hidden purpose not as readily obvious.

Herrnstein and Murray by conducting attention toward scientific reasons for racial inferiority inherent in African Americans, obscure the most threatening issue. That issue is that too many African American males and females have become well educated since the passage of the Civil Rights Bill. More African American males than ever are graduating from high school in spite of the widely reported statistic that more black young men are in jail than in college. African American females out distance the males in college. Affirmative Action, maligned as reverse discrimination, has white college students attacking black college students because they believe the black student is taking their white counterpart's place in class. Furthermore, when African Americans excel in college, they are a threat to whites after graduation in the shrinking job market. And as in all situations, black males are the major threat to white males. But whites must face the fact that even though they have thrown every obstacle they can come up with to destroy African American males, it's like Sterling Brown said, "Strong men keep a coming! Strong black men just keep a coming! Strong black men!"

The Bell Curve is a conspiratorial document which rationalized the proposed "Contract for America." Although the Contract would have hurt whites and blacks, blacks usually suffer more because they have lower income, education, housing and medical care. Low and no income black men, in particular, are hit hard because they are already operating in a deficit. In addition, black mothers tossed off welfare are causing many children to suffer, more are homeless, neglected and abused. The danger is in the intent of the Herrnstein-Murray crown who control financing of institutions and influence political decisions.

The Bell Curve is designated as the definitive research on black inferiority designed to obliterate struggles by black people to overcome centuries of racism in America. Legislators have gone so far as to pass a bill to end protection against illegal searches and seizures in certain instances; black men are most likely to be the victims of this change if it becomes law. Black welfare recipients are the images used to inflame passions when in fact more whites will be removed from the rolls.

Furthermore, the code words *welfare mom, single parent households* were evident in the debates surrounding the welfare issue. The undercurrent was the motivation to also cut out any welfare money that the women might share with African American men. "Able bodied men" to be swept from the welfare roles, are code words for *black*. Increased campaigns would have merit if socially disadvantaged black men were gainfully employed and able to support their children.

The main reason for African American men being absent from the home is the lack of job stability. An inherent male characteristic is the inclination to provide for his family, but when prevented from living up to that tendency many men walk away from home. Societal standards, women and the men themselves usually adhere to the material values of this society. When they can't be obtained, and there are no adjustments, agreements or ways out, some men give up trying. Of course, there are the plain out and out dead beats; they exist in every race and every society. But in this picture is the Catch 22: poor education and miseducation, unemployment, racism, wrong values, etc. land African American men and youth in jails and keep many from the roles of fathers, husbands and providers. None of these reasons are caused by inherent racial inferiority as *The Bell Curve* would have you believe.

Underlying these negative conditions are the four fears of white men. Since men are the major concern of white men, publishing literature and using mass media to portray black men's perceived adversary as inherently inferior is another racist, convoluted way of addressing white male fears by attempting to make black men less than human. Herrnstein and Murray are not as crude as some of the earlier bigots, but *The Bell Curve* is the SAME OLD BULL CURVE. It's just a new book with the old smell.

4
Atrocities

Charles Pollard got $25, a certificate and a picture after twenty-five years of being an unwitting subject of the infamous Tuskegee Experiment, a drawn out Nazi death camp type experiment that lasted for forty years and involved 400 African American men![1] Mr. Pollard had syphilis that was purposely left untreated by the government as part of an experiment to watch African American men slowly suffer, infect their mates and offspring and die so their bodies could be autopsied. Allegedly it was to see if African American men and white men with syphilis were different. Yet, no comparable program was created for white men.

Pollard said he and the other men who lived in Tuskegee, Alabama, were subjects in the infamous Tuskegee syphilis experiment from 1932-1972, meeting in black churches commandeered into clinics for over twenty-five years. A black nurse, Eunice Rivers, enticed the men into joining the experiment. Over the years she kept tabs on them for the Public Health Department, later the Centers for Disease Control, the sponsors. The church, the preacher, the teacher, the doctor and the nurse were trusted and revered in the black community sixty years ago. If someone wanted cooperation in the black community they were the sources for allies. With their support no one suspected a conspiracy by a government sponsored experiment and a trusted black nurse.

The United States Public Health Service and the American Medical Association, according to documented records, conducted life threatening experiments on the black men that caused untold physical and mental problems for them, their wives and offspring for unknown generations to come.[2] This horrific experiment was carried on in a conspiracy of silence until a white public health investigator, Peter J. Buxton, came across the scheme. Even then, it took him seven years to get it out in public. It was not until he convinced a reporter to break the story that the experiment was halted.

Buxton, appearing on Tony Brown's Black Journal, Channel 12, Philadelphia, PA, October 1994, gave updated information.[3] He said he had written his bosses and their superiors to complain about the experiments. They were astonished that he would think of asking them to take action to halt the experiment. After many months, the public health officials held a conference at their Atlanta, GA headquarters. Buxton said he was subjected to a "blistering private attack."[4] He was told the black men in the experiment were "volunteers, it was to benefit their race, and something they should be proud of."[5]

All along doctors had been writing papers on the experiment for the medical profession and not one doctor was on record as objecting. Buxton read to the Atlanta meeting their own published research, "In all cases morbidity was worse in their [the black men in Tuskegee] group compared to a control group."[6] Suddenly, Buxton said, "a light went on."[7] One doctor claimed the article under his name was written by someone else. Then they tried to clear up their participation. But the decision was made to continue the experiments until the black men died and were autopsied.

Furthermore, in Buxton's travels he heard of a patient in the experiment who went insane. His family took him to a doctor unbeknownst to the public health doctors. When the outside doctor's tests revealed syphilis, he ordered penicillin, and the man was cured. However, when the Medical Society heard about it, Buxton said, "They jumped on the doctor, and told him he was supposed to let the man die so that he could be autopsied. He had messed up their study they told the doctor."[8]

The historically damning reason for the Nazi like experiment was "to see if syphilis affected black men different from white men."[9] Buxton and the doctors emphasized they did not infect or inject the black men with syphilis. However, when penicillin became available after 1943, they continued to refuse to treat the victims. The doctors allegedly said the black men in their experiment had "late syphilis" by then, and the theory was that it was less infectious.

Nurse Rivers, as she was known, did not think she was duped when asked if she had been lied to by the authorities. She maintained in a televised interview that she was innocent and believed the government was sincere in the experiment. "Her statements supporting them is bunk," said Buxton.[10] He categorized her as a "tragic figure." He also noted that other blacks were involved, as well as whites, as lab technicians and doctors.

When asked by Tony Brown if this was a unique case of medical racialism because "there's a general belief that blacks are genetically inferior to whites," Buxton weakened his case by saying it's not just blacks that are used for experiments; it could be going on right now in orphanages and asylums.[11] He said the Tuskegee experiment was not the same as the Nazis' because they did not inject and kill people to see the results. The Americans gave them a slow painful death and allowed infection of their wives and possible genetic abnormalities in their descendants.

Buxton made another startling revelation on the telecast. He said that six months ago a friend who is a professor of surgery told him he had implanted a device in a patient (race unknown). He, in turn, told another surgeon in Germany. Instead of being appalled, the German asked for a half a dozen; he said he would put them in Turks (their minority). (Buxton did not explain why he and his American doctor friend were appalled at his actions in America, or why the device was implanted.)[12]

The issue of experiments on living humans is gaining more and more publicity. Furthermore, it is bringing science fiction to life. Due to the frightening conspiracy to destroy black boys and men, it is not unreasonable to believe that more experimentation is taking place in prisons, hospitals and the armed services. The use of Ritalin, a dangerous drug to control behavior, is widely believed to be overprescribed for black boys.

An even more spine chilling report is the story of an African American man showing an X-ray photograph of a device implanted in his head while he was incarcerated.[13] Devices to "tag" cattle and humans, relative to the surgeon's confession, was reported in a newspaper published in Albuquerque, New Mexico, July 16, 1994. The device is the size of a grain of rice, patent number 5,042,826, the Injectable Transponder TX1400L. The article quotes the patent office: "The primary object of this invention is to provide a system for identifying an object, animal or person, consisting essentially of two units: one being a passive integrated transponder (PIT) which is carried by or embedded in the thing or animal to be identified and which responds to interrogation with an identifying code, and the other unit being an interrogator-reader separate from the PIT."[14]

The Colorado-based company that makes the implant is Destron. Their literature says the implant has an injectable transponder and describes the implant as

> ...a passive radio frequency identification tag, designed to work in conjunction with a compatible radio frequency ID reading system. It has a pre programmed chip with a unique ID code that cannot be altered; over 34 billion individual numbers are available. When the transponder is activated by a low frequency radio signal, it transmits the ID code to the reading system. It takes a twelve gauge needle, weighs 0.002 ounces and it has an operating frequency of 125 kHz.... The INFOdex System Model HS5700L1 Intelli-Reader scans the animal ID and enters the data into software via keyboard. Simply down load the information and print the report. Even easier, the mini

portable reader transmits the ID number into the computer for the operator once the information is stored in the computer memory.[15]

"Could part of the interest in getting our children immunized to the point of requiring smart cards for each one to be part of the machinery to get them all tagged? It would only take the cooperation of doctors, and many of the children get their shots from the state. Even private practitioners can be leveraged into doing what the AMA decrees."[16] At the present time, there is a nationwide campaign spearheaded by President William Clinton to have children immunized at birth. Who is monitoring the vaccine contents and dispensers?

The article reminds the public that military people can be injected without knowing for what; the public lines up for flu shots, immunizations, etc. "It would be easy to tag citizens and keep them on file like cattle in a herd."[17]

In a related incident in *The Sunday Sun*, 1993, a New York City publication, Brian Wronge, a 33-year-old African American, residing in Brooklyn, NY, charges that while he was incarcerated he was implanted with a paramagnetic computer chip in his head and body in October of 1987.[18] Arrows point to the implants in Wronge's head in the accompanying photograph in the article.

Wronge reported to *The City Sun* that his troubles started when he was isolated from the rest of the prison population and suddenly experienced difficulty breathing. Although he was in good health, worked out with weights, had no previous problems with breathing, and had a normal chest X-ray, he was sent to Billy Seaton Hospital's pulmonary clinic. He was convinced that he should undergo a bronchoscopy, usually conducted under a local anesthetic. Instead, he said he was "knocked out completely" and awoke on a respirator and intravenous equipment. He had a pain in the back of his throat and surgeons told him he had suffered cardiac arrest during the procedure.[19]

After he was released from the hospital, Wronge experienced a series of physical ailments, and "it quickly became apparent to Wronge that something was terribly amiss."[20] He suffered from dizziness, nausea, incontinence, headaches and insomnia. Some of the symptoms subsided over the next few years but curious things continued to happen sporadically. At times he would hear a mechanical-sounding voice in his ears repeatedly saying things like, "your mother doesn't love you" or "your family will be killed."[21]

Wronge had obtained an associate's degree in prison and had researched a paper for a psychology course discussing how the human senses can be imitated using computer analog devices. He recalled that after he got a high grade for that paper he started having problems in the prison. Subsequently, he was shuffled around, he believes, in an attempt to build a criminal and psychiatric profile and "to discredit any charges he might make in the future."[22]

Wronge said he began to suspect that whatever had been done to him was for the purpose of experimentation and observation. He began to fear that he might be harmed because he wasn't reacting as anticipated and stepped up his efforts to get discharged. Success came in May 1989, but due to the side effects of the implanted chip, Wronge said he suffered from short term memory loss. This landed him back in jail for parole violation when he missed his check-in appointment.

In Elmira prison, Wronge worked in the offices and had access to grievance committee files. He said, "I saw several documents detailing complaints from inmates about the discomfort they were experiencing in their ears and oral pharynx—that is, the area at the back of the throat."[23] When they complained, "almost uniformly, they were sent to the 'satellite unit', an area of isolation...for mentally unstable inmates."[24] Buoyed by the documentation and armed with information that his case was not unique, Wronge, upon release, immediately sought medical advice. "He went to see Dr. Albert O. Duncan, a physician...who wrote a prescription for an MRI, a type of x-ray."[25]

Diagnostic Imaging Associates, a Brooklyn lab, reported back: "MRI of the chest was performed...These images reveal the presence of a paramagnetic foreign body artifact noted in the region of the left anterior chest wall at the level of the axilla..."[26] Wronge also consulted a neurologist who had worked with his mother, Dr. Jayesh Kamdar. After relating his story, Kamdar referred him to a Manhattan diagnostic lab for a CAT Scan. The resulting report from MRI-CT Scanning Inc. revealed: "The bilateral external canals demonstrated dense rectangular shaped metal foreign objects. The etiology of this finding is uncertain. Clinical correlation is suggested."[27]

Wronge was referred to surgeons to remove the micro chips but he could not afford the operation. This proved to be a blessing, however. Because he was unemployed and had been in mental hospitals while imprisoned, Wronge applied for Social Security Disability—Supplemental Security Income (SSI). The government's response said he did not qualify because their investigation of the psychiatric records disclosed that his claim could not be substantiated by hospital records.

This startling piece of information made it clear to Wronge that prison officials and medical personnel had, in fact, sent him to these facilities solely for the purposes he suspected. Wronge said, "They tried to destroy my head and then make it look like I was the one who was crazy if I attempted to expose them. We all know if you go around saying you hear voices—immediately you are a nut. It is set up that way."[28]

Wronge searched around to find people to help him in his efforts to expose what had happened to him. Among them were the Reverend Phil Valentine, Director of the Institute for Self-Mastery, and several physicians who asked to remain anonymous. On examining Wronge's ears they saw "a flat metallic object like a computer chip covering a portion of his eardrum...where I should have been able to see straight through the area of the sinuses," one doctor said.[29]

The City Sun's interview with the anonymous physician said that Wronge's assertion that something was placed in his throat, was not observed. However, he said, "The larynx is a tube that opens and closes depending on pitch. I suspect they can open the membrane and insert a chip right there where the voice box is located. This would enable someone on the other end of a microwave transmission to monitor Wronge's speech and even thoughts. Remember that saying, 'You can't go to jail for what you think'? Well not anymore," said the doctor.[30]

Wronge is pursuing the case through the courts, according to *The City Sun*, and he testified over WHAT-AM radio in Philadelphia, Pennsylvania in 1994. A physician Wronge consulted to have the chip removed, spoke to *The City Sun* and corroborated the findings of other medical authorities. However, Wronge had problems with physicians and attorneys taking his case because it is too controversial.

He said he believes they are experimenting with people in prisons and mental institutions to see how they react to psychological trauma. "Young black males particularly are targeted and brought into the penal system for political and other reasons. Once they have you in the government's custody, they can do these biological and psychological studies without their permission; knowledge of the practice is widespread and not limited to African American men."[31] However, since they are more likely to be in situations that expose them to experimentation, such as prison, the armed forces, and given the climate of increased efforts to maintain white superiority by demonizing and destroying black men, it is a growing area of concern and need for militant watchfulness.

When Brian Wronge was asked if he had concern for his personal safety, he replied, "They have disrespected my temple and for all I know may have tried to kill me. I am a soldier at war."[32] Reverend Valentine feels that "if they try to do anything to Brian it would validate what he is saying. They would prefer for him to look unstable. We have to protect Brian. If we do, we are only protecting ourselves."[33]

Experiments

It was commonplace after a visit to the health clinic for an African patient to proudly describe to family and friends his rare ailment. The doctor had called in all his colleagues to examine the patient. The poor and the unsophisticated patient thought it was preferential treatment, and although that's the nature of clinics, sometimes it is a painful or humiliating experience. What's worse is the history of immoral mistreatment sometimes ending in murder in research experiments created for African American victims. Many were coerced, frightened and uninformed when going along with the experiments. The gallery of horrors contains evidence of experiments on African Americans and others, but due to the second class status of the majority of African Americans throughout the years, they were subjected to most atrocities. Major offenders were the public health agencies and hospital clinics.

An article in *"Z" Magazine* entitled "Medical Repression" reports a number of shocking incidents involving racist medical procedures and experiments on African Americans recorded since the 1930s. "Z" states: "Moreover, one might also feel that whereas the issue of informed consent was a highly questionable practice fifty, forty or even thirty years ago, surely it is not an issue now. Unfortunately, this is not the case."[34]

The article sites the plutonium experiments by the U.S. Government that reveal "a disturbingly large involvement of people of color, especially African Americans."[35] Although this story deals with African American men and youths, African American women are equally abused by government and private medical research.

At least 300 African Americans, mostly women, were involved in fifteen studies by Tulane University researchers at Charity Hospital, states "Z". The subjects were required to swallow radioactive capsules, were injected with radioactive mercury into laboratory created blisters that were intentionally cut open. They endured 118 degree heat and intentional diarrhea. Supposedly, the studies were to see the effect of mercury on people with congestive heart failure, but none of the black patients had the disease, according to the "Z" article.[36]

Scores of guinea pig research studies around the U.S. are done on African American women, with and without their consent. The drug Norplant, a device implanted in a woman's arm to prevent pregnancy was heralded by white supremacists in and out of the media as the answer to high birth rates among poor black women. During the research phase, it was disclosed that half the women dropped out of the study because of side effects, and no projection was developed to predict the long term effects of the drug on women or on their babies when they come off the drug. Now in some states, judges require black women to take Norplant or lose public assistance.Dilantin is also a drug that was tested on black women without their knowledge to study the effects in women having cesarean sections, charges "Z".[37]

No one knows precisely how long and how much experimentation involves African American men, women and children. Nevertheless, it is common knowledge amongst black people that we are the most studied and researched humans on earth. Primarily, as documented throughout, it is due to white's fears which revolve around the issues delineated in this book.

In the military, servicemen belong to the government, it is believed they can be exposed to any type of research without their consent or knowledge. It is the same in prisons, say prisoners.A twelve-year military study showed that sixty-one African Americans were guinea pigs in a study by the University of Cincinnati Medical Center.[38] The military personnel and twelve others were exposed to full and partial body radiation ten times higher than normal. After sixty days of exposure to the radiation (250 rads in one session), twenty-five of the patients died. These "tests were conducted from 1960 to 1972, by Eugene L. Saenger, an eminent radiological health specialist....Ironically, Saenger also serves as a key government witness on radiation lawsuit cases brought against the Department of Energy." Dr. David S. Egilman, researching the Cincinnati experiments said, "What they did was murder those black patients."[39] He testified before the House of Representatives Energy and Power Subcommittee that the experiments had no informed consent and were not ethical.

"Z" states that in this society "blacks' lives are easily expendable."[40] The radiation experiments rife during the Cold War were not limited to blacks; however, "they do show a continuing legacy of medical science using unsuspecting African Americans. There is little or no informed consent involved."[41]

In The Oakridge Experiment, back in 1945, a 55-year-old black truck driver, Ebb Cade, was admitted to the U.S. Army Manhattan Engineer District Hospital for injuries received in an auto accident.[42]

He was not expected to live, and on April 10, 1945, he was injected with a significant amount of plutonium. Cade was the first of eighteen to be injected; he received 0.29 micro curies of plutonium 239, a dose equal to 1,030 rems or 41.2 times what the average person receives in a lifetime! Dr. Robert Stone, who gave the injection, is alleged to have told Dr. Karl Morgan, a physicist, that Dr. Stone was "particularly concerned because, this poor 'expected casualty' had suddenly gotten up out of his bed and disappeared."[43] Stone also claimed to be disturbed because "the black man was unconscious and not expected to live when given the plutonium, could not have given his consent to be a guinea pig, and I was afraid he was selected for this experiment in part because he was black and it was unlikely any of his family would learn of the plutonium injection..."[44] There is no record of what eventually happened to Ed Cabe. What influenced him to escape in his condition? What superhuman strength did he dredge up to escape from this doctor Frankenstein's experiment? Did he survive, and if he did, what condition was he in and did he contaminate his family or others?

Another case concerned an African American Pullman porter, Elmer Allen, who was in a freak accident on a train.[45] His injured leg was diagnosed as a fracture at first, then a lesion and finally bone cancer. An amputation was recommended, but three days before he was given an injection of plutonium 238 in the muscle of the leg at the University of California Hospital. Although Allen's injection was smaller than the dosage given to the eighteen other subjects, his dose was "hotter" and is more radioactive than plutonium 239. Furthermore, because of Allen's amputation, approximately half of the plutonium 238 stayed in the remaining leg, resulting in his receiving six times the radiation for the average person. Officials who designed the study lied when they said Allen was informed and signed a consent form. A 1974 follow-up investigation by the Atomic Energy Commission found that patients were not told plutonium was being injected in their bodies. (Allen was told he was receiving a radioactive substance.) Allen lived many years afterwards. Again, with what physical conditions was he forced to live with?

Also, abominable crimes against African Americans were perpetrated outside hospitals. In 1951, the U.S. Army secretly contaminated the Norfolk Naval Supply Center. Alexander Cockburn, in *The Nation*, stated that a ship with infectious bacteria was reported as one of the types chosen because blacks were more susceptible to it than whites.[46] He also reported that in 1960 an Army Chemical Corps experiment with mosquitoes with yellow fever and dengue fever were dispersed in Savannah, Georgia and Avon Park, Florida, over an exclusive black area. African Americans reported fevers, bronchitis, typhoid, encephalitis, stillbirths and mysterious deaths.

"Z" concludes, "The scientific establishment conveniently forgets informed consent and our government funds medical and scientific research that harms and murders innocent and unsuspecting civilians in the name of National Security." The Cold War radiation experiments along with all the other known and unknown experiments are just one more part of the sad history of Africans and African Americans where the medical profession forgets its basic tenet: "Do no harm."[47]

The National Institute of Mental Health Addiction Research Center from 1953 to 1958 did experiments on black patients giving them LSD.[48] The racist medical researchers did not spare babies and in 1953 and 1954 seven newborn black babies were injected with radioactive iodide in John Gaston Hospital, in Memphis, TN. No follow-up on their health was done and John Gofman, a leading scientist on the effects of low level radiation and professor emeritus at the University of California, Berkeley, said the children had increased risk of cancer and "to do nothing is criminal. Equally ominous is that five other similar experiments were carried out in Detroit, Michigan; Omaha, Nebraska; Little Rock, Arkansas; and Iowa City, Iowa, with a total of 235 newborns and older infants experimented on."[49]

Dr. O.J. Andy, a neurosurgeon in Mississippi, performed brain surgery that destroyed part of the thalamus (an organ that analyzes sensations and governs feeling) on African American children who were termed aggressive and hyperactive. Operations were performed on children as young as six.

"In the 60s, the National Institute of Mental Health and the Justice Department funded research that looked into ways biomedical controls (i.e. brain surgery, genetic theories of violence prediction and control, behavior modification, to name a few) could be used to curb violence in the inner city—the black community."[50] Three Harvard professors made the startling proposal that psycho surgery could be used to control not only urban rioters but some black leaders allegedly suffering from brain damage and dysfunction. In fact, these proposals were discussed in Congress for a series of violence centers throughout the U.S.

Carrying on the racist legacy, in 1992, Dr. Frederick Goodwin, one of the nation's leading psychiatrist, formerly head of the U.S. Health and Human Services Department's Alcohol, Drug Abuse and Mental Health Administration, speaking to the National Mental Health Advisory said that youth violence was his number one priority. He said his department was looking into areas to control violence and aggression through family studies. "...Goodwin said the inner city had lost some of its civilizing evolutionary things;" therefore "...it isn't just careless use of the word when people call certain areas of certain cities jungles."[51] Goodwin capped the insults with "hyper aggressive and monkeys who kill each other are also hypersexual" (one of the main hypotheses of this book—the fear of black male sexuality).[52]

The program Goodwin proposed, a $400 million federal research grant, was shelved (temporarily) after black professionals and others raised a furor over his remarks. He was demoted to head of the National Institute of Mental Health. "Z" states, "He is still head of NIMH and many questions regarding the direction of the various research projects under the umbrella of the Violence Initiative go unanswered."[53] Furthermore, labeling violence a health issue is reaping huge sums of grant and medical care funds. It is suspected that the health records of the black victims and offenders from this approach to violence land on Goodwin's desk and will be used against African Americans, particularly males based upon Goodwin's past record.

5

Injustices and Imprisonment

Making the connections between the Four Fears of white men and their devastating impact on African American men is critical to understanding the fallout which affects many facets of black men's lives regardless of their class. Some aspect of the Four Fears is found in every vital issue involved in the lives of black men and youths and has serious implications for their families and society in general. Examples include: discrimination in general, in entertainment, courts, law, the glass ceiling in corporations, civil service jobs, academe, construction work, homelessness, economics (legal and illegal), health care, mental health, family matters, and housing. Discrimination in police methods, the legal system, economics, employment, and education is the main reason for the excessive imprisonment of African American men and youth.

The most egregious atrocity is unjust sentencing and lack of rehabilitation. First, it must be understood that African Americans are victimized from crime on both sides—the criminals and the "injustice system." Thus, the community pays because they bear the brunt and because they are in the untenable position of often siding with criminals because of the injustices in law enforcement and the courts.

Under the apartheid practiced in this country, great African American men have been unjustly sentenced to jail, as if they were nothing more than a common criminal or a railroaded brother. Look back to any time in U.S. history to observe the truth of the matter: Marcus Garvey, Malcolm X, Martin Luther King, George Jackson, Huey Newton, W.E.B. DuBois (indicted).

Criminal, rapist, prisoner, drug dealer, robber, burglar—all are words synonymous with black man. When a crime is committed, it is often assumed that the perpetrator is a black man. "A Black Man Did It" is widely charged because people know the police will believe them. A recent example is the heinous crime committed by Susan Smith, a South Carolina woman who murdered her two babies by drowning them in her car because she was spurned by her boyfriend. Smith told police a black man hijacked her car and kidnapped her toddler boys No African American man in America was safe from persecution until she confessed. Crying, "A Black Man Did It," has been a common practice down through the ages, sending unknown numbers of black men to jail or death.

It is a shameful fact that America has never confessed guilt nor apologized before the world for its intransigence. On the contrary, prodigious efforts are made to depict black men as inferior with a proclivity to commit crime; therefore, it is justifiable to warehouse them to protect society. Black men are locked in cages, shut behind bars to insure whites that their greatest fears will not become facts. As explained in this book, the Four Fears are kept in check by imprisonment, executions, and conditions created whereby the disadvantaged kill each other, die early, have poor health care, become unproductive, or are rendered docile and acquiescent. Those African Americans who perpetuate struggle against the unjust system and force changes have limited powers because of the unrelenting oppressive tactics of the majority. However, if it were not for those who toil despite the oppression, black people would still be in slavery.

Playing out the role of racism and capitalism on the road to fascism and genocide, white, right and religious misfits, along with black conservative lackies have Republicrats, the Congress, legislatures, National Rifle Association (NRA) and its handmaiden the gun lobby manufacturers and municipalities marshaled for an all out attack on black men. The related prison culture has industries bursting at the seams making millions from taxpayers to construct and supply prisons. They take tax money away from much needed schools in places like Chester, PA, one of the most devastated cities in the United States, to train prison guards.

Opening the throttle in the rush to use black men as scapegoats for the economic and social ills, the infamous chain gangs have returned with mostly black men and youths shackled on road gangs. They do slave labor with the sun beating down on them in summer, and suffer the icy blasts of winter, twelve hours a day, with guards' shotguns trained on them. The prisoners who rebel are shackled to a stock to stand in the blazing sun all day as their ancestors were punished during slavery. A beefy-faced, redneck warden in an Alabama prison echoed the historic fear of white men—black males' sexuality—when he said, "I don't care as long as my momma or your momma is not getting raped or robbed."

The other purpose is psychological devastation. Humiliating and dehumanizing African American men is ingrained in historic white supremacy tactics. Placing black men in chains before the public is the diabolic motivation. Make a special note that these are not the hardened murderers and violent offenders, they are the short term, young non-violent offenders. Obviously, the objective is to demean them, make them angry and hardened so they will turn into vicious criminals, to be executed or fill up the new prisons to support the economy.

A few whites are on the chain gang to sanctify the modern practice to include poor whites to disavow racist intent. This game is well known among African Americans. Media knows that they show white prisoners to convince the public there's equal treatment.

The majority of the African American offenders committed petty crimes, yet came under felony statutes. Therefore, their third offense mandated life imprisonment. A television program showed a white boy who strangled a person, and burned the body to obliterate fingerprints—he was given twenty-five years because he had no prior record. A black man who had not robbed, raped or murdered anyone was given life because he had two minor convictions. The sentencing judge said he was required by law to hand down the sentence. When questioned about the outcome of the ruling, the judge said he had been sentencing men for eighteen years and locking up everyone hasn't helped.

When a television program did a story on the reinstitution of the chain gang, a well known moderator laughed about it and the reporter said, "It was a good idea." The White Racist Press (WRP) can always be counted on to indoctrinate the masses to accept the wishes of the white supremacists and the corporate interests.

The prison economy in human misery is a four billion dollar industry. A "Prison Expo" showed hyped up, grinning salesmen and women demonstrating high tech security, special toilets that can't be stopped up and all sorts of locking devices. One white male expo demonstrator said, "...got a gorilla pushing on the lock (imagery of black men)...he can't budge it." It costs nine million dollars a year to run one prison. Therefore, cutting down on staff, which takes 80 percent of the budget, was the spin on the expo sales pitches pushing the latest in hardware technology. An ominous portend came from a statement by a white male who said, "One of the most difficult things is spending money on the less productive people in society." Speculation on the next step makes his observation ominous. After the profits from the hardware are pocketed by the leeches, the cost of maintaining the prisons and the prisoners overrides the profits for the communities, and the hardened offenders come out angry and revengeful, then the next step is to exterminate them. One Alabama juror recommended, "Create a Devil's Island (a notorious French penal colony), give them some seeds and hoe." These are the seeds of implanting the idea of genocide in the minds of the public. Will other means be fomented to relieve society of the burden of prison costs? Will mystery prison diseases erupt, will there be more experiments on prisoners, more suicides, more victims of crimes as prisoners are cut off from humanizing programs, more vicious reprisals, or Attica type riots occur?

But, one can hear the voice of Frederic Douglass saying, "...for a man to keep me in a hole, he has to stay down here with me to watch me." As the society tries to destroy the black man, it destroys itself. The various militia numbering 400,000 and the bombing of the Federal Building in Oklahoma City, murdering 168 people are testimonies to the coming apart of America as white supremacists arm to prevent people of color from obtaining equality.

The return of the chain gang and forcing prisoners to work without compensation is a direct throw back to early legal practices in the U.S. in the 1600s.

> Although slavery was not legally sanctioned until 1641, records dating as early as 1636 reveal that the Puritans had already evolved their own version of local slavery. Initially, the local slavery system was penal. Servitude could be imposed as punishment for a variety of crimes ranging from robbery to nonpayment of fines; servitude imposed

as punishment was usually labeled "slavery" by the Massachusetts colonial courts.[1]

From the beginning of the prison system in the United States, African Americans have been disproportionately locked up, both men and women. In *Criminalizing A Race*, Charsee McIntyre recounts that the Western World had initially invented imprisonment for common law offenses allegedly to reform criminals. In early societies prisons were for revenge or preventive detention while awaiting execution.[2]

"In the new United States, African Americans suffered under both approaches, the new and the old, and often found themselves imprisoned for no apparent nor understandable reason."[3] It is contended here that the "no apparent nor understandable reason" was the Four Fears of white men—the belief that black men must be contained and controlled has been the underlying motivation since the inception of the prison system in the United States.

In the 19th century, a sympathetic English chronicler who nevertheless viewed African Americans as inferior, lower caste members, wrote to American abolitionists that he inspected prisons in the North and found that "unemployment, lack of education, and prejudiced witnesses and juries combined to insure the extraordinary large African American inmate population."[4] It is the same today, even as we approach the year 2000. McIntyre goes on to document that "prejudice, and economic depression assured free African Americans' incarceration and poorhouses. Yet, friends and foes cited crime and prison statistics to create a stereotypical characterization of African Americans as debased, depraved, and inherently criminal."[5] Thus, the belief was concretized from the very start in the North and supported justification for slavery in the South.

Those free, unemployed African Americans were defined as vagrants; therefore, they were imprisoned. Again, today it is the same case, except indoctrination and identification with the oppressor encourages behavior that leads many forcibly unemployed, largely due to the Four Fears, to commit "unlawful" acts to survive. Just as today, those unable to pay costs and fines had added sentences. Another significant racist law was that all African Americans were subjected to curfews—being caught out late at night or visiting was a crime! Not showing deference to whites, looking at white women directly or suggestively, entertaining, drinking, congregating, and sex outside of marriage were crimes and subject to imprisonment. Such extremely picayune infractions were to address the inordinate fears of black men and at the same time to support the prison economy.

In the cauldron of racialism surviving since 1636, the vicious cycle, "Catch-22" situations, decrees that the less jobs for African American men and youths, the more criminal activity, the more imprisonment, the more public outcry about the costs, the more the public sanctions slave labor.

Review the historical records and it is blatantly clear that the Four Fears over the years have been the underlying cause of the African American male (and female) struggling to escape the bottom of the "melting pot," for them a cauldron. Short reprieves brought about during war time boom economy soon reverted back to business as usual once the economy took a downturn. Therefore, it is very easy to make the case that there has never been a sustained period of economic growth for African Americans, and African American men suffer dramatic reversals, as mentioned above, but keep in mind too the related ignored effects on African American women and families.

Most of the disorder among African Americans caught in the vicissitudes of racism and economic instability is laid at the feet of the Four Fears and its relationship to the certain plight of African American men. The litany of atrocities has a new member, the "Crack Law." Linn Washington, cites that the get tough law by Congress is so outrageous that some federal judges are balking at their mandate. "Blacks comprised 78 percent of the persons receiving the death penalty under the federal drug kingpin statute between 1988 and 1994 although three quarters of those convicted under the same statute were white. ...Blacks are nearly 93 percent of those convicted in federal courts for use and or sale of crack cocaine yet whites compromise 2/3 of

America's crack users. According to federal statistics....Nearly three quarters of the mainly white first time offenders convicted in federal court for powder cocaine possession get probation compared to less than one third of the blacks convicted for crack possession, stated a federal report issued this year."[6] Linn says, "Crack War Racism" is a crime itself.

The crime rate according to the FBI fell in 1992, the first time since 1984, yet since 1980, there has been a steady increase in blacks sentenced to death. Although blacks are 13 percent of the population, 114 were sentenced to death in 1992 compared to 147 whites.[7]

The *Statistical Abstract of the United States 1994* reports information not broadcast nor widely known: 1992, eighteen whites and eleven blacks were executed by the Army (again disproportionate to the numbers enrolled). Between 1930 and 1980, 405 African Americans and just forty-eight whites were executed for rape.[8]

In 1993, nearly 70 percent of black males graduated from high school compared to 18.2 percent in 1960. However, 25.7 percent white males finished college but only 11.9% black males. These statistics expose the lies about black males obtaining privileges from race based scholarships and Affirmative Action. There has been a 6.3 percent increase in white males finishing college since 1960.

Health statistics reveal the potential for sustaining life for African American males: it is a gloomy picture. In nearly all the primary causes of death in the U.S., they are in the lead and have the lowest life expectancy, both the underprivileged class and the middle class: 65.5 years compared to black females 73.9 years, white male 73.2 years and white females 79.7. Projections for the year 2000 portend black males slipping to 65.3, while black females rise to 75.1, white males to 74.3 and white females to 80.9 years.[9] Black males, therefore, on the whole, do not receive the benefits of their contributions to Social Security. Here again, they are the victims of the forces that prevent them from living as long as other groups.

6
Sports And Athletes

African American Sports Giants

Fear of African American men's strength and intelligence overlaps when it comes to sports. Executing and maneuvering requires left brain intellect in several sports. Logistic capabilities together with right brain creativity and innovation, along with proficient imagery and synergism in other areas have created the distinguished record of great African and African American athletes. When allowed the opportunity, African and African American athletes excel in every sport. Racist propaganda and racial stereotyping have been utilized to discredit African Americans in sports as in all other endeavors. However, in sports, greater lengths have been taken to discredit black men because of their publicly demonstrated physical and mental superiority, and allusions to sexual superiority. In addition, boxing implies the execution of anger. Before the exposure of the lies, routinely black men were depicted as physical brutes with low mental capabilities.

Arthur Ashe in his landmark research makes a point of the fact that Africans came to America as warrior athletes. He starts his definitive publication, *A Hard Road to Glory*, by reporting on Egypt (actually Ancient Kemit) where tombs, pottery and art are evidence that Africans engaged in sports recorded as early as 2200 B.C.[1] Sports activities included boxing, fencing, swimming, rowing, archery, jumping, racing, wrestling and horsemanship. Religious documents mention ball games too. Ashe says that when Europeans finally reached Africa they found that Africans already had their own sports and games for their physical and psychological survival. No doubt too, many of the traditional rituals that the ignorant Europeans observed and reported as pagan ceremonies, involved activities of physical nature similar to recognized sports. "They (Europeans) found sports already ritualistically woven into the social fabric of African daily life," according to Ashe.[2]

Most contests were connected with religious ceremonies, fertility and rites of passage rituals or for entertainment of visitors. This was contrary to the European experience where the church dominated all aspects of life. After the bloody, savage Roman sports had tainted sports, the church heavy-handedly regulated sports activities. On the other hand, Africans were freely engaging in their centuries old practices as they interacted with nature, animals and humans for spiritual growth and development, as well as mind and body development. Racing, stick fighting, bow and arrow prowess, wrestling, gymnastics, tug-of-war, swimming, climbing, riding, spear throwing, and dancing were regular activities.

Enslaved African captives in America found their athletic abilities constrained by their Calvinistic captors' religious convictions. Nevertheless, despite the harsh prohibitions visited upon the sons and daughters of Africa, and the Native Americans, they managed to engage in contests in their limited leisure time. They boxed, and wrestled, fought mock stick battles and played ball games. It is a tribute to the Africans that their superior physical and mental strength enabled them to endure the slavery holocaust and still have sufficient strength, will and determination to engage in sports for leisure.

Among the manifold insults to African Americans, then and now, the State of Virginia passed a law in 1705 permitting owners to list people (slaves) as property. "Black horse trainers were among the first to be listed."[3] As property they had no rights. Their skills, handed down from their African ancestors, enabled white slave holders to use them to make untold thousands of dollars.

Africa's natives were the first great American jockeys. "Proscribed by race, servitude, and class from initial participation, black jockeys later became the very model for the profession. They performed so well that their white peers felt threatened and arranged for their eviction from the profession. But the records established leave no doubt of their superior accomplishments."[4]

Black athletes out performed other races in every sport when allowed to compete. In order to continue justification for dehumanizing African Americans after slavery was abolished by law, white American scholars led the way in spurious research, reporting that they and the Bible proved that Africans were inferior to white men in the structure of both mind and body. Along with these specious religious/historical reports, was the equally stupid assumption that whites were stronger than blacks. Therefore, they had to invent ways to prove their assumption when they were confronted with black superiority. Herbert Spencer, a noted white supremacist scientist, tried to use statistics to prove that blacks were inferior because their brains were allegedly smaller than whites'.

Spencer was among the "new scientists" who failed to disassociate themselves from their preconceptions about African Americans. Spencer was known as a social Darwinist, and his cohorts stopped quoting Darwin and quoted him instead. Using hit-and-miss techniques they engaged in racist misuse of science.[5] This movement gained momentum during boxing champ, Jack Johnson's era. It was a period of heightened bigotry that rehashed all of the racial inferiority claims. The new scientists took up the cause of Dr. J.H. Van Evrie. In 1853, he wrote *Negroes and Negro Slavery—The First Inferior Race*. Reaction to Reconstruction brought forth a book published by Biblehouse Publishing Company, *The Negro a Beast*, by C. Carroll.

Newby says the scientists "unconscionably exploited science and social sciences. They drew heavily on theories and research as they interpreted them, eugenics, genetics, ethology, biology, psychology, physiology, anthropology, sociology, geography as they assembled a formidable array of scientific and pseudo scientific evidence to support their cause."[6]

Because the twentieth century was to be the age of science, racists felt compelled to give their racist ideas an "elaborate scientific rationale." In a continuation, academic and scientific opinion continued from the nineteenth to the twentieth century to be against African Americans. "The achievement of scientific racism was to strengthen the popular prejudice by clothing it in a mantle of academic and scholarly authority."[7] Jim Crow's Defense has 450 references in books, periodicals and journals regarding so-called Negro inferiority and intelligence! (See *The Bell Curve* , Same Old Bull Curve.)

Sports, as mentioned before, became the focal point for attempting to prove the inferiority of black men because as Arthur Ashe said, "Conventional white thought needed some excuses for why blacks were excelling in sports."[8]

Going back to England in the history of boxing, Ashe reports that white boxers often adopted aliases so that if they lost a bout to a black boxer they would not be embarrassed by that public knowledge. The adoption of a ring name came from this early white reaction to their fear of being inferior to blacks.[9]

William Richmond, a free black man, born on Staten Island in 1763, grew up on the docks of New York City during the British occupation. A British Manhattan commander noticed Richmond who often got into fights with sailors, but rarely lost. Percy asked Richmond's mother to allow him to take him to England. He got into his first fight unexpectedly when a white man accosted him. Richmond whipped him soundly and that led to more challenges as the sport gained popularity. He racked up an impressive record of wins and gained an opportunity to fight the white champion, Tom Cribb. The bout took place on October 9, 1805, with nobility and commoners shoulder to shoulder in a festive atmosphere. English honor and white superiority were at risk and thousands showed up to see this landmark battle.

Cribb beat Richmond, and the newspapers reported "a black man had been put in his place."[10] From then on the superiority of the white race was always at stake when a black and white fighter competed. The same situation prevails in other sports through the ages. Therefore, it is difficult to assess sports solely on merit when whites and blacks compete because of the race issue and all of its related aspects that impinge on the outcome of the event: the effect on the participants, the financial, social and political factors.

Richmond, the first athlete to contest for a national or world title in any sport, eventually groomed a black protégé who beat Cribb, but racist dirty tricks robbed the young man of his win. Tom Molineaux, born under slavery in Georgetown, in Washington, D.C. in 1784, was the son of a boxer. Tom's brothers also boxed and their master, Algernon Molineaux, won so much money on them staging bouts between slaves on neighboring plantations that he freed Tom when he won a large wager on him. Tom took the measly $500 Molineaux gave him from the thousands he made on him and his brothers and went to England. In London, he met Richmond and trained under him. After winning six fights, Molineaux challenged Richmond's nemesis, Cribb. December 10, 1810, was a rainy and cold day, but no fight in memory had attracted as much attention.

After twenty-seven rounds, the bout was in doubt, but in the twenty eighth round Molineaux hit Cribb with a hard right and he went down. Cribb failed to "toe the mark" after thirty seconds, and Molineaux and Richmond jumped with joy. However, a dirty trick by an official soon cut short their glee. Cribb's aide jumped into the ring and accused Molineaux of hiding weights in his hands. The officials then waived the rules and allowed Cribb a full two minutes to revive. Cribb and Molineaux went sixteen more rounds and Cribb was declared the winner. The rules were thrown aside to defend white English honor. An added insult was that Cribb was paid two thousand dollars and Molineaux had to settle for a collection from the crowd.

Dejected and disheartened, Molineaux and Richmond were the first victims of racism on record, as white supremacy was instituted in boxing. The psychological toll on Richmond and Molineaux and other black sportsmen is rarely taken into consideration when judging their behavior. For example, Molineaux wrote a self-effacing letter to Cribb asking for another bout that, nevertheless, exposed the racial prejudice he faced: "I cannot omit the opportunity of expressing a confident hope that the circumstances of my being of a different color than that of a people amongst whom I have sought protection will not in any way operate to my prejudice."[11] Cribb agreed to the fight, but oddly Molineaux started drinking and arguing with his benefactor, Richmond, which caused them to part. Before the fight, Molineaux ate a whole chicken and downed it with a quart of ale just before entering the ring. Cribb easily beat him. He went downhill after that and died a penniless alcoholic in Ireland, never again to see his family back in America.

Richmond, on the other hand, suffering the ignominy of losing to Cribb and then seeing his protégé have his win stolen out from under him, nevertheless, proved his superiority by continuing giving boxing lessons to several well known black boxers, operating the tavern he owned and fighting his last fight at age fifty-two. Looking at Molineaux and Richmond's response to the devastating treatment they received, raises the question: did the fact that Molineaux was born into slavery and Richmond was born free make a difference in their response to adversity?

Boxing

The treatment of African Americans in the sport of boxing is clear evidence of the enormous, historical fear white men have of black men. The white champion boxers refused to fight black fighters. Racism was the reason they feared the white supremacy myth would be exposed. Black boxers were reduced in some instances to pleading with the likes of John Sullivan and Jim Corbett for matches. Peter Jackson, a black boxer, ended one missive by reminding Corbett that "if a man is faint-hearted he should never step over the ropes."[12] He was thirty-two and still hoping for a match with Corbett, who had promised Jackson a match but then reneged. After Jackson's prime was passed, Corbett wrote in his autobiography that Jackson was the best fighter he had ever seen.

Ever the vanguard of racism, the white press in 1895 in a letter written by white sports editor Charles A. Dana in the influential *New York Sun*, attempted to instigate whites to save white race superiority. Dana wrote: "We are in the midst of a growing menace. The black man is rapidly forging to the front ranks in athletics, especially in the field of fisticuffs. We are in the midst of a black rise against white supremacy....Less than a year ago, Peter Jackson could have whipped the world—Corbett, (Robert Fitzsimmons)...but the white race was saved from having at the head of pugilism a Negro....There are two

Negroes in the ring today who can trash any white man breathing in their respective classes…George Dixon…and Joe Walcott (Jersey Joe Walcott's father)… If the Negro is capable of developing such prowess in those divisions of boxing, what is going to stop him from making the same progress in the heavier ranks?"[13]

Dana went on to excoriate his white readers, taunting them with, "Is it because they are far better than their white brethren or is the white race deteriorating? Wake up you pugilists of the white race! Are you going to permit yourself to be passed by the black race?"[14] This level of gutter sports journalism was designed to rankle whites and to beef up racist hatred toward black men, particularly in sports where they were matchless.

Johnson, Joe Walcott (the first) and Joe Gans epitomized "The Hard Road to Glory" for black fighters. Outrageous, unthinkable, despicable crimes were vented on these men. Gans and Walcott were subjected to threats on their lives, causing them to allegedly throw fights out of fear. Black boxers in this era had to endure fouls, clouts to the head while down, referees who were hit by white boxers when they ruled in a black boxer's favor, outright robbery of their purses and outlandish rules such as Gans having to reduce to the 133-pound limit at age thirty-two; on the day of the fight, he also had to make the weight in his boxing clothes and he received only $11,000 from a $34,000 purse. His opponent's manager took advantage of him because he was strapped for money. Fighting under the brutal Nevada sun, Gans vomited four times and broke his hand in the 32nd round. Twice he picked up his opponent after knocking him down only to have him hit a vicious blow below the belt in the 42nd round. The referee awarded Gans the fight on the foul and he regained his world lightweight title.

Gans' victory stirred racial violence against black people across the country. These racist attacks were the first serious outbreaks in boxing against black people, followed by numerous attacks by whites in sheets and without sheets. They were bound to protect white supremacy and white economic power.

Jack Johnson

Born in Galveston, Texas, March 31, 1878, Jack Johnson was the first black man to win a championship from a white man in the United States.[15] Because of recalcitrant racism, the world will never know how great he could have been. Johnson was a man with a fifth grade education and a "Ph.D." in boxing and body. However, fighting the rampant bigotry and prejudice affected this son of the mighty warriors of the Karomantee tribe of West Africa in ways we will never know. We can only surmise from some of his self-defeating behavior the hardships he endured as he bucked the system that was dedicated to emasculating and annihilating him.

Johnson became a target of racists because he did two unforgivable things in the United States: he beat a white man at boxing, dispelling the myth of racial superiority, and he married white women, evoking the most troubling fear of white men—black men's sexual superiority. As was the case with Johnson's predecessor Joe Gans, the first African American to win a world boxing title, winning championships meant Johnson lived in fear of being attacked, beaten or possibly even killed. As a black fighter, he had to shoulder this additional burden.

Johnson was denied matches and contradictory excuses were publicized that he, like all black men, was a coward, yet the white fighters ran from fights with him.[16] The so-called great white boxer John L.

Sullivan had set the tone in the world of boxing by espousing his racism, and others followed in cooperating to maintain boxing as a bastion of white supremacy.[17]

From a young man, Johnson developed into his own person early on seeking his own way in life. Running away at thirteen resulted in being abused by whites in the many odd jobs he had to undertake in order to survive. This evolved into resentment, frustration and a seething anger.[18] He started boxing for a living but again had to suffer the indignity of battles royal: fights with more than two combatants with the last man on his feet declared the winner. In another ignominious situation, his first serious bout with Joe Choynsky, a Polish-Jewish boxer, Johnson was KO'd in three rounds, but both he and his opponent spent three weeks in jail because boxing was illegal in Texas. Ironically while in jail, Johnson took boxing lessons from Choynsky.[19]

One way white managers down through the years got their hooks into black boxers was by forcing blacks to have white managers in order to book their fights. Many of the managers became multi millionaires on the backs of the dependent black boxers, while most of the boxers died penniless. Jack Johnson's attitude and great physical ability agitated whites in boxing as well, but greed won out and they booked him. Johnson was disliked before he scored his championship wins in boxing, and his wins over white women, because he was considered uppity. He had the temerity to publicly harangue a Canadian boxer, Tommy Burns, who ran all over the world making excuses and trying to duck a bout with him. When Burns finally stopped running and agreed to fight him, Johnson opened his training before the public and shocked them by outrunning a kangaroo.[20]

At the fight, two well known racial adversaries were the ringside reporters: hard-core racists John L. Sullivan, guest commentator for the *New York Times* and Jack London, *Call of the Wild* fame.[21] If Johnson had not won decisively, the news would have been the perverse reports of these two staunch defenders of white manhood. But, Johnson whipped Burns soundly, and London sent out a written wail for Jim Jefferies, hiding out on his farm. "Jim…must emerge…and remove the golden smile from Johnson's face. Jeff it's up to you!"[22]

Now Johnson added another insult to the whipping he gave Burns: he started cavorting with white women. He also started engaging in self-defeating behavior that helped to undo him. He was arrested in London twice for breaking furniture and using foul language. Meanwhile, the white world was scurrying about furiously looking for their "great white hope."[23]

Jim Jefferies reluctantly agreed to come out of hiding and fight Johnson. Immediately, Jefferies and other white agitators started calling Johnson "yellow" in public.[24] Imagine what they called him in private. Johnson added to the instigator's defilement when he was arrested in New York for attacking a black man. He also fired his manager. Pressure came down from religious groups, and the fight with Jefferies was canceled, but the Nevada governor agreed to have it in Reno and an arena was built in a record three days.[25]

Jefferies fired up the antagonism with a statement in Reno that he realized that the white race was depending on him to defend its athletic superiority. The world press sent out communiqués daily, thirty thousand people came, tickets went for ten to fifty dollars, and the scalpers plied their under-the-table trade. In the ring, the traditional handshake was eliminated, a blatant insult to Johnson. Johnson, ironically, wore trunks with an American flag draped through the belt loops. Jefferies attempted the near impossible—he hadn't fought in nearly six years, but before he had been unbeaten in twenty-one fights.[26] Nevertheless, due to racism he was the favorite. Johnson toyed with Jefferies and taunted his cronies by yelling slurs at them during the clinches. By the eleventh round Jefferies was spitting blood and hugging Johnson at every chance he could wangle. "Jefferies knew that if he fell at the feet of a black man it would symbolize the failure of the white race. The myth of the natural superiority of the white man of the black man had brought Jefferies out of retirement…now he was paying the price. In round thirteen Jefferies was a pitiful sight as Johnson allowed Jefferies to hit him at will while laughing at his feeble attempts."[27]

Finally Johnson's blows caused Jefferies' supporters to beg Johnson not to hit him any more. Johnson ignored them and hit him again until Jefferies sank to the floor. The referee was still counting, but Jefferies' handlers rushed into the ring in clear violation of the rules to help Jefferies to recoup. Finally, the referee gave Johnson the fight. Johnson, as the undisputed world heavyweight champion rubbed it in. He said he won the fight because he outclassed Jefferies in every department. Johnson received $106,000 and Jefferies $90,400; with no federal or state income taxes to pay, both cleaned up.[28]

Johnson's win led to hell breaking loose in many quarters. Hundreds of black men were killed and beaten by mobs, some nearly lynched by angry white retaliation.[29] Many major cities banned films of the fight, and Congress went so far as to pass a law banning distribution of films across state lines for commercial purposes. The US government did not want a film of a black man whipping a white man shown across the country.[30]

From that time on Johnson was hounded and attacked by whites with government sanction and assistance. He married three white women. The first time he was accused of transporting a white woman across state lines for immoral purposes, a violation of a federal statute, the Mann Act.[31] Johnson was railroaded by the very judge who was the cause of keeping black men out of major league baseball, Kennesaw Mountain Landis.[32] Johnson was convicted when a former white suitor joined in the prosecution against him. He was sentenced to a year and a day and fined a thousand dollars. Johnson's reaction was to contrive an elaborate escape plan; he fled the United States for the next seven years, all because the racist superiority myth had been killed.[33]

Johnson went from country to country, fighting, winning, losing, and getting into trouble as he went. He was even charged with throwing an important fight with Jess Willard in 1914. Johnson later said he was forced to throw the fight as the price for getting back into the United States.[34] Returning to the United States, he served eight months of his sentence at the federal penitentiary at Leavenworth. Ashe says, "He was the most dominant force in all of boxing for the first twenty years of this century. Nearly every non partisan expert agrees that had he not been forced into exile, he would have had as fine a record as Joe Louis. That he was hounded for his choice in women was, on the one hand, unfortunate for him, but on the other hand, more a testament to the miscarriages of America's ideals of equality, fair play and justice."[35]

Jackson's and Jefferies' lives ended with a turn of events similar to the ending for Joe Louis and Max Schmeling. Before his death, Joe Louis was a sorry sight—poor and broken, photographed being pushed in a wheel chair by Max Schmeling, a rich German business-man whom he had defeated in a world renowned championship fight. Louis didn't make the error of running after white women; however, he was the personification of all the white man's fears regarding black men. Instead, he was punished via the Internal Revenue Service. Louis had been a political sports pawn in the pre war United States and Germany's cold war. His fights with German Max Schmeling, like Jesse Owens' track victory, were used for United States propaganda against Hitler. Then during the Second World War, Louis, a loyal black American, had lost forty-six months of his boxing life by serving in the Army. Discharged at thirty-two, his best boxing days were over, he had traveled 70,000 miles, visited 5,000 servicemen and given ninety-six exhibition fights. Moreover, he had volunteered to do it. Furthermore, he had to face and fight discrimination against him while in the Army in the United States and England. Finally, he was given a Legion of Merit Medal for his "exceptionally meritorious conduct." Yet the IRS said he still owed them $80,000 in back taxes, and even took $600 his mother left him in her will. Because he was a black man he got the whipping from Uncle Sam outside the ring that his white opponents could not give him inside the ring. His money troubles became exhausting and pushed him downhill. Finally, an act of Congress halted the tax billing, but they never wiped it off the books. He never recouped, and died broke. While Schmeling and Jefferies died wealthy old men, Johnson after suffering many injustices died in an auto acci-dent in 1946.

It was not until Joe Louis came along in the 1930s that a boxer captured the attention that Jack Johnson had garnered. White supremacy is still a significant issue when the contenders are mixed. While Louis was not vilified as Johnson had been, he was the victim of bad financial advice and prejudice, and he said in his autobiography, *Joe Louis: My Life*, "I know I caught hell all during my career because I was black."[36]

Muhammad Ali

Muhammad Ali exemplifies the fears white men exude regarding African American men. Although he was not seen keeping company with white women, he was still a sexual threat to whites. Ali had a clean cut, handsome face and golden body along with mental brilliance, sharp wit, and shiploads of charisma. A non-smoker, non-drinker, non-drug user, Ali brought back to boxing the audacity of Jack Johnson, without his weakness for white women. During his forced exile from boxing for refusing to enter the army during the Vietnam War, Ali was offered $400,000 to play Johnson in a film. He turned down the offer because he said he didn't want to play the role of a black man chasing white women, or to glorify white women because they allow themselves to be used as symbols of white supremacy.

Ali erased the traditional, humble, dim wit image of boxers. Yes, he said, "I'm beautiful, I'm the greatest." The jealous white media dubbed him "the Louisville Lip," but black people greatly admired him, he was refreshing.

The Kentucky Golden Gloves Champion at age fourteen, fought his way to the heavyweight championship over Sonny Liston when sports writers, like their predecessors, were still calling black athletes animals. Ali quotes an Englishmen who described Liston as "a savage glaring eyed gorilla with mighty muscles..."[37] By Ali declaring he was pretty, and he is, they were hard pressed to criticize him physically.

However, the demonization switched from physical degradation to religious degradation. Ali joined the Nation of Islam, named by the white press "a hate race sect" and "the black Muslims," the name that has stuck to make it sound more sinister.

Carrying on another tradition Liston was not only depicted as an animal by the press, the Senate Kefauver Committee investigating crime put out rumors that Liston was tied to the Mafia. In *My Own Story*, by Ali, Kefauver said if Liston won the fight they faced the ugly prospect of having the World Championship revert to mob control. Ali retorted, "I was to find that they considered it a worse prospect to have it under 'black Muslim' control."[38] They would rather have had the white Mafia than the black Muslims in control of a champion fighter.

After Ali won the championship and announced his membership in the "Nation of Islam," he was deferred from the draft because he failed the entrance test. This sparked an uproar. In one case, a Georgia lawyer started a "Draft That Nigger Clay" campaign. Again, as the Congress historically does to noble black men who dare to buck the system, they considered calling for Senate hearings because of Ali's religious affiliation.

Eventually, the forces arrayed against him succeeded in reclassifying him 1 A. Then he refused to fight in Vietnam because of his religion. His decision brought down a fire storm of attacks on him: "It was as though I had touched an electric switch that let loose the pent-up hatred and bitterness that a big section of white America had long wanted to unleash on me for all my cockiness and boasting, for declaring myself 'The Greatest' without waiting for their kind approval. For branding their Christianity a farce and flaunting my own religion, for preaching among my own people without apology, a 'black-is-best' philosophy."[39]

In 1967, he received a five-year sentence for refusing induction; it was reversed in 1970. When he won his case he said the only people to thank were his manager, lawyer, law professors at Columbia University and a lawyer for the Legal Defense Fund of the NAACP.

Also in another area long in contention, Ali bucked a tradition that interfered in the cash flow to interests outside his camp.

> Since the first day I decided to become a fighter, I challenged the old system in which managers, promoters or owners looked upon fighters as brutes without brains. But when I first came into boxing, tied up as it was with gangster control and licensed robbers, fighters were not supposed to be human or intelligent. Two animals to tear each other's skin, break each other's nose, and bleed and bleed, then get out of sight while the managers and the lawyers and the promoters announced it all, judged it all and profited most from it....They could call me arrogant, cocky, conceited, immodest, a loud-mouth, a braggart, but I would change the image of the fighter in the eyes of the world...."[40]

Ali said he and only one other fighter who had won the heavyweight championship were not invited to the White House by the President. The other fighter was Jack Johnson. Twenty heads of state invited Ali to their countries, but not his own President because of religious differences in a country that preaches religious tolerance.

First the World Boxing Association and then the New York Boxing Commission lifted his license. It took seven long years for him to regain it. Ali endured vicious attacks in person, through the mail and by phone. After his exile from boxing, just before a fight in Atlanta, Georgia he was sent a package containing a black Chihuahua with his head severed, wrapped in a confederate flag. A note read, "We know how to handle black draft dodging dogs in Georgia."[41] In addition, Ali's training camp was besieged and he was shot at from ambush.

Once again, as in the case of Jack Johnson, the government interceded in order to prevent an African American man from reaching his full potential in his profession. Black men must be contained at any price no matter how unfair the tactic, because it is the American ethos—keep white supremacy alive.

O.J. Simpson

The Four Fears of black men are also the underlying reason for the hysteria perpetuated by the mass media and the majority in the O.J. Simpson murder case. Simpson was tried and acquitted of the murders of his ex-wife, Nicole Brown Simpson, and "her friend," Ron Goldman, at her home in Los Angeles, California in June of 1994. Simpson was the embodiment of the Four Fears: intelligent, strong, a sex symbol, and since the murders, portrayed by the white media and the prosecution as driven to kill by anger. The media became white society's voyeurs, peeking in the window of O.J.'s and Nicole's life. They revealed every facet of their existence and were titillated by every detail of their intimate life—what do they really do—white women and black men? Aside from wars or a president's assassination, O.J. Simpson, one lone black man, caused more national and international furor than any event in American history.

O.J. Simpson, former media icon, loved by millions, black and white, nicknamed "The Juice" by adoring football and movie fans, was a Heisman Trophy winner, former Buffalo Bills all pro, University of Southern California all star running back, movie star, football TV commentator and Hertz Auto pitchman—a real African American hero. For his reward, Simpson was given a trophy—*a white woman.* Many black male professionals, sports and movie personalities prefer white women over black women. But Simpson's trophy status was rescinded when he was charged with Nicole's murder. Then he became just another black male under arrest, presumed to be guilty of everything, including murder, spousal abuse, rape, etc.

Simpson's acquittal unleashed outrage in volcanic proportions unseen in modern times. A national lynch mob, egged on by the mass media was hell bent on destroying Simpson. All semblance of respect for the Constitution, the Bill of Rights, democracy, the jury system, and fairness was thrown out the window. This book convincingly demonstrates that nothing draws more gut responses from whites than a black man who has sex with and allegedly abuses his white "trophy." The resentment lurks under a scab of fear and anger that when jostled spews venom. Committed to avenging Nicole's murder, the vigilantes used cyberspace techniques, but they had the supremacists' mentality of their ancestors. In fact, it was reported in the press that a white female group actually called for Simpson's lynching.

President William Clinton, who is quick to call for sanctions against black people, such as Louis Farrakhan, Sister Souljah, etc., hurriedly declared a "Domestic Violence Awareness Week" in a knee jerk reaction to make O. J. the poster "Boy" for abuse against women. The Million Man March at the nation's capital was the largest Washington demonstration in history, with the exception of Vietnam protests. Clinton scurried out of town to Texas where he made a watered-down speech on racial harmony, and took a swipe at Minister Louis Farrakhan, march organizer and leader of the Nation of Islam. Coming on October 16, 1995, just a few days after the Simpson verdict, October 3, 1995, no doubt Clinton feared the ire of whites if he supported the march and appeared to care about what blacks felt. When the deep-seated, widespread division of whites and blacks spilled out, Clinton said he was "surprised by the depth of the divergence in so many areas." It is impeachable that the President is "surprised" at the most serious problem that has existed for centuries in the U.S. largely because of Americans' fears of the potential power of African American men.

The television news across the nation orchestrated the demonstrations of the reactions to the Simpson verdict. Throughout the trial they broadcast scorecards of blacks' and whites' answers to questions about Simpson's guilt or innocence. When the verdict was imminent, the news media positioned their cameras where all white or all black viewers were stationed. And while reactions of blacks and whites split along racial lines, the media posturing helped to exacerbate the situation. In truth, there were significant numbers of African Americans who believed Simpson guilty and whites who believed him innocent. In addition, the media set up contributed to the belief that African Americans condoned his behavior and his lifestyle. That response is due to the racial biases and stereotypes that lump all black people together. African Americans are as diverse as any other racial group, however, they are likely to respond as one when it comes to the justice system. The American system has a damning, documented record of injustice toward African American men, so when there is a reasonable doubt, as in the Simpson trial evidence, African Americans tend to come down on the side of the accused—in this case that was labeled the "Trial of the Century." The Simpson trial should be called yet another case in the "Century of the Trial of African American Men."

Most whites are in denial about racism and maintain an accusatory frame of reference reserved for the average African American man because of fear and jealousy. Racial issues are evaded, downplayed, discredited and ignored. If you tell the average white person of some personal racist incident that happened to a black person, the white person will always say, "Oh, that happens to us too." By trivializing, or disclaiming individual responsibility for racism, it can safely be ignored until confronted. The latest pejorative slogan is to accuse African Americans of "playing the race card" when racism is pointed out in a situation. Simpson's trial, it was charged, was prejudiced by his attorneys because they "played the race card." In reality, the race card was played from the very start when Simpson, a black man, dated Nicole, a white woman. To whites, the "race card" means using racism for an advantage in a contested issue. Blacks see it as a factual necessity to be addressed to keep the record straight. After Mark Fuhrman, who discovered the primary evidence against Simpson, was heard on tape using the word *nigger* forty-two times, bragging about planting evidence, beating minority prisoners to a pulp with blood running down the walls that had to be hosed down along with the cops, was the defense team to ignore the evidence? When other evidence indicated that Simpson's blood was planted in his home and the bloody glove did not fit him in the courtroom demonstration, were these matters also to be disregarded in order not to expose Fuhrman for what he is? Furthermore, it is patently racist to suggest that African Americans are so unintelligent and emotional that introducing evidence of race makes them incapable of rendering an unbiased decision. Actually what whites are accusing blacks of is the way they, whites, respond to issues of race with vindictiveness and revenge. The trial symbolized race. Whenever you have an African-American on trial for the murder of white people, race is an inescapable part of the trial.

Because of the mania over a prominent black man accused of murdering his young, white, blond wife, during the sensational trial, information and speculation were broadcast around the globe for unprecedented hours daily. Every tid-bit of information was hashed over and made the subjects of programs, comedy routines, sermons, debates, portends for future trials, threats and speculation. As an outgrowth of the trial, entirely new show formats were developed. The case was a bigger story than the elections and the very important National Health Care debate promoted by First Lady, Hillary Clinton. Judge Lance Ito had to recess court early to prevent the Simpson trial from stealing viewers away from President Clinton's State of the Union Address. Furthermore, when the verdict was about to be rendered, President Clinton stopped working in the White House, Congress recessed important committee meetings, businesses and schools halted as the world awaited the verdict.

Over one hundred and fifty cameras and twice as many reporters had kept a vigil outside the Los Angeles courthouse during the trial as the world became a wired global village to all the proceedings. Acting like wild animals moving in for the kill, reporters dogged witnesses, attorneys, and anyone else with the hint of an attachment to the case. Twenty-seven thousand stories were filed during the first year of the case and over 1000 pieces of evidence were gathered by the prosecution to try to convict Simpson. Vending of anything that resembled him or the case was hawked on the streets outside where demonstrations for and against him included numerous types of attention getting, bizarre Los Angeles antics that went on every day.

Inside, in the red light of the television camera's eye the posturing and acting for the world to see influenced and shaped the judicial process. Every word and gesture by Simpson, jurors, lawyers, Judge Lance Ito, witnesses, clerks, sheriffs, and spectators made news. Insignificant things such as the fresh flowers in the courtroom and Judge Ito's use of gigantic hourglasses were more fodder for news. Prosecutor Marcia Clark's hairdo, that was changed twice after the trial from a greasy looking gherri curl, to a frizzy floozie style to a conservative, straightened, lawyerly Joan of Arc style, made the press. Clark was reported to have asked for more alimony to purchase an expensive wardrobe for the cameras. Lawyers were decked out every day in different, gaudy attention-getting ties and California colored suits. A spectator who won the lottery for a seat went into a gospel moan loudly thanking Jesus before the camera; well into the trial, a person was seen being taken out of the courtroom by sheriffs because it was alleged to be a man dressed as a woman.

For once, however, the viewers were able to see how the media can manufacture news. Those viewers who watched the trial could see that the media edited and reported the proceedings so that the clips they showed were not always a true reflection of what was going on in the trial. Also, some of the expert commentators contradicted what was shown.

Ironically, O.J. Simpson was the most composed person during the entire trial. Except for an occasional grimace, he was stoic. Under the unrelenting camera's focus, even while hearing the searing testimony and seeing the grisly death scenes of his former wife and her friend, generally he remained calm. Without commenting on his guilt or innocence, Simpson demonstrated the level of strength that whites fear in black men. In addition, on camera, and in his brilliant defense strategy, O.J.'s attorney, Johnnie Cochran was the master of the drama and legal wit. The never-before-shown-to-the-world expertise, brilliance, intelligence, strength and good looks of the African American men involved in the case were a major factor in the seething anger and outrage demonstrated, especially by white men, such as Ron Goldman's father. The defense led by Cochran caused the prosecution in desperation to use defense witnesses for their rebuttal questions. The "Dream Team" strategies had the legal eagle television commentators squaring off and trying to explain what was going on to the viewers.

Those white Americans who still believe they are African Americans' masters and make it their business to decide what should be done to black people to control and keep them in their place, had a field day blaming and prophesying what to do and what to expect after the trial. For example: they said the police failed Nicole because they mollycoddled Simpson; the federal government should step in and charge Simpson with violating Nicole's civil rights; the trial was blamed for sales slumps in shopping malls across the U.S.; the case would increase calls for gun control; it would cause whites to lose faith in the power of the police; there would be a major shift to the right if Simpson were acquitted; it would cause Affirmative Action to be dumped.

They were correct on some scores, and in fact, the retaliation against the verdict spread far beyond Simpson. In the hate filled aftermath of the decision many black students, including children were verbally attacked by their teachers. Some black people were threatened with losing their jobs as tensions mounted in the workplace and some whites stopped speaking to African Americans. The white backlash fomented a wave of grass roots' action without any leadership promotion. Liberals joined bigots, in marches and protests with ugly racist slogans, vigils, boycotts; telephone banks sprang up to organize anti-Simpson verdict activity. Threats to insure that welfare, Affirmative Action, and social services to African Americans were cut off filled the air from the cess pools of verbalized racism in America—talk radio.

An editorial page article in the *Philadelphia Inquirer* after the verdict said the American jury system should be done away with because "our jury system isn't sacrosanct; there are better ways to justice...juries have always abused the institution, sacrificing impartial justice to political or ethnic goals. Today urban black juries all too often put race above justice."[42] (The author Michael Lind cunningly omitted the sordid 400 year history of legal injustices against African Americans including the all white jury not guilty verdict in the Los Angeles cops beating, caught on tape, of Rodney King.) These truths are the history behind the "them against us" reaction of some African Americans. Land advocates an autocratic, "small number of professional and lay judges."[43] Or, he asks, had Simpson "been tried under civil law...would it have degenerated into an appalling spectacle of dirty tricks and bizarre legal hairsplitting. How likely is it that Johnnie Cochran would have played the race card...?"[44] Lind exposes how much he is actually in sympathy with autocratic laws while saying that his way would prevent an alienated public from "...understandable pessimism (which) might be support for plebiscitary rule in politics and, perhaps, vigilantism in law enforcement."[45] Historically, when matters involve African American men, Land and his ilk call for drastic measures, even go as far as to advocate changing the laws.

Although Simpson's media named "Dream Team" had all white male attorneys except for Cochran and Carl Douglas, all of the attacks on the defense were made against Cochran. White defense attorney F. Lee Bailey got racist, rogue cop Mark Fuhrman to lie on the witness stand saying he had never used the word *nigger* in ten years. The exposure became a pivotal factor in the jury's decision. Furthermore, white defense attorney Barry Scheck meticulously exposed and whittled away the flaws in the investigation. Nevertheless, they were never personally attacked and vilified as was Cochran; some even attacked Cochran more vehemently than Simpson.

An all out blitzkrieg was waged on Simpson to destroy him. He was sued in civil court by Nicole's and Ron Goldman's relatives. The Brown and Goldman families were understandably distraught. However,

Simpson financially supported the entire Brown family; helping the father to get a Hertz car franchise, sending Nicole's sisters to college, loaning them money, taking them on trips, and buying Nicole a condo before marriage. If Nicole was beaten and stalked by Simpson over the many years of their marriage as was claimed, certainly the Brown's share the guilt. Ron Goldman's father, "doeth protest too much." The reasons for his estrangement from Ron were covered over, it was rumored that he didn't like Ron's life style. Ron's birth mother did not raise him and she was divorced from Goldman, yet she got in on the suit. Goldman went into a frenzy when Cochran ran up points in the summation arguments and ran for the cameras shouting that Cochran was "a whore" to compare Mark Fuhrman to Hitler. He also bellowed that Cochran was a sick man who should be put away. His vicious, unwarranted castigation of Cochran, an officer of the court, was never discussed in the media and Goldman was never chastised. In addition, it was barely reported that Goldman and Fuhrman had the same attorney during the trial. Evidently a black man, no matter what his profession or status, can be disrespected by anyone of any status in the media without fear of criticism. Defense Attorney Bob Shapiro, who made one million dollars defending Simpson, took sides with Goldman over the Hitler remark. Shapiro had also fallen out with F. Lee Bailey after Bailey maneuvered Fuhrman into perjuring himself on the witness stand. Shapiro wanted to avoid the race issue. The breach between Shapiro and Bailey over the issue was deep and after that Shapiro testified against Bailey, the godfather of his child, in another case helping to get him sentenced to jail! (Bailey represented Claude DuBoc who pleaded guilty to drug conspiracy and money laundering; a federal judge held Bailey in contempt for misusing DuBoc's money.) Was this retaliation against Bailey for his critical role in the Simpson case that ripped the covers off more police misconduct, even after the Rodney King beating disclosure, for all the world to see?

The African American women jurors came under the most reprehensible attacks. Nevertheless, they remained dignified, well composed, articulate, thoughtful, and intelligent when grilled on television and for the press. Having made great sacrifices, sequestered for a year and having received only a tiny stipend, they came under scathing, demeaning, bigoted attacks for the verdict. Protest signs carried by white women said: "Next time give them an I.Q. test before the trial. They don't know the difference between DNA and SAT." Those women protesters were no different from the women who hide under the sheets and march with the male members of the Ku Klux Klan. The black women's detractors said they were too stupid to understand science, although the jurors said they understood and liked Barry Scheck's DNA explanations the most. Patronizing whites said they just did not understand abuse, another way of saying they were too dumb to know that being beaten by a man is wrong.

The black women were not to blame for the verdict. Marcia Clark and her bosses outsmarted themselves by skewing the jury selection to a majority female jury because of the abuse charges against Simpson. The prosecutors were more concerned about the issue of a black man and a white woman than the danger of putting a known racist cop on the stand to testify against the defendant. The LAPD had a reputation of getting away with murder against black men. The D.A.'s office was so accustomed to complicity in policy lying on defendants and disregarding the complaints of the community about police brutality and frame ups, that even after the Rodney King decision they remained arrogant about their power. Furthermore, their ignorance and arrogance had them believing that black women have the same white feminists ethos as theirs. What this writer has been saying for years in regard to the Four Fears is that our problem as black people is the way this society treats black men. Black women's lives would improve dramatically if whites would stop trying to destroy black men. Much of the abuse that black women endure from men is because of black men's frustrations and anger caused by the injustices in this society. Furthermore, black women realize that it is not just their husbands' and lovers' behavior that affects them. They are also affected by their sons, brothers, uncles, and male cousins who live under the specter of white supremacy due to the Four Fears. African American mothers, mates and wives are always "waiting to exhale" when their sons and mates are in the street, either because of the police, or the crimes created by institutional racism.

As Simpson watched his fortunes dissipate, because he did not testify in his behalf on the advice of his attorneys, he resorted to his conditioning and made a video to tell his side of the story. However, a huge public outcry ensued and groups organized against the sales, although thirty or more books had already been churned out, and a movie or television series was in the making. Some newspapers, television, radio, and advertisers who also profited from the case condemned him for "trying to make money off the murders." What were the Goldman's and Brown's doing but making money off the murders? The most onerous, hypocritical reaction to the verdicts were the stations and publications who refused Simpson's ads. In addition, an organized movement across the U.S. jammed Simpson's 800 number to prevent purchasing the tape around the clock. It was a First Amendment issue and some mediums respected it, but others did not.

Simpson came under more heat than any man in memory except Hitler. He has been told he's not wanted in his favorite white restaurants and golf clubs, neighbors have asked him to move, and he has received death threats. Overall he was turned into the Salman Rushdie (Islamic author sentenced to death and hiding in exile for a book critical of the faith) of the U.S.

There was a blatant difference in the public outrage and hostility toward Simpson, compared to the alleged perpetrators of the fiendish, cowardly bombing of the federal building in Oklahoma in 1995, during the trial. Simpson, a black man was charged with killing one white woman and one white man while suspects, Timothy McVeigh and Terry Nichols, two white men were arrested for killing 168 people including over twenty-five babies in the daycare facility. Early reports broadcast across media said that the Nation of Islam and Minister Farrakhan or Arab terrorists were responsible. That rumor led to the harassment and death of an innocent Arab American citizen. After the initial reporting on McVeigh and Nichols' affiliations, the alleged bombers were rarely in the news except for trial preparations. Moreover, the alleged culprits are reported to be members of white racist militia groups numbering 400,000 weapon carrying members, with the averred purpose of revenge and the overthrow of the U.S. government. Compared to the public outpouring of vitriol against Simpson, there's been little more than weak expressions of shock that their own kind did the dastardly bombing in the heartland of America.

While the Simpson trial was on, evidence of racial injustice practiced by the notorious LAPD and Mark Fuhrman were exposed in similar historic patterns of police abuse of African American men and women in New York, Philadelphia, Louisiana and Texas. Yet these patterns were buried in the self righteous chest beating over the not guilty verdict. Instead of venting anger over one incident, examining the larger national problem of police misconduct over the years and working out solutions was lost and the opportunity to bridge the gulf was crushed. Exposure of the bigger problem unveiled the festering racial division in America and the Simpson case was used as an excuse to make those who enjoy the fruits of white supremacy and fear the potential power of African American men even madder. The unspoken reason they were madder is because black men, Simpson and his attorneys, one steeped in jurisprudence and the other one rich, used their (white's) system of justice to obtain justice. But, the more the covers are pulled off fascism the worse it gets. Simpson's verdict and the Million Man March on Washington—ridiculed and the lowered crowd size reported by the National Park Service exposed as a lie—coming in the same month created more fear and hatred of African Men. It could have been fields of healing planted if the majority were in favor of it, but the African American man and men of color must be destroyed because of the Four Fears.

The tidal wave of outrage over Simpson's acquittal propelled the Brown and Goldman families to hire top lawyers to pursue a victory in a civil suit. October 23, 1996, the trial got underway in Santa Monica, California.

Racial aspects of the cases–criminal and civil–reflected each other in some significant ways. The verdicts, the courtroom cameras and circus atmosphere in the first trial were different. The judge in each case was an Asian: Judge Lance Ito in the criminal trial and Judge Hiroshi Fujisaki in the civil trial. It was rumored that the selection of an Asian judge was to offset accusations of racial bias. The locations were mirrored opposites: the criminal trial was in downtown Los Angeles and the jury was predominantly African American. The civil trial was held in outlying Santa Monica, and the jury was predominantly white. The "objective" white media had made much of the fact that the L.A. jury was predominantly black but rarely mentioned that the Santa Monica jury was predominantly white. Furthermore, some of the anchors and reporters referred to Simpson as a murderer, influencing public opinion notwithstanding the fact that he was acquitted of murder. The media, and that segment of the public that lives in the land of denial, about race caterwauled when race was brought out as an issue in the criminal trial, yet not much was said about Fujisaki not allowing race evidence into the trial. Nor did he allow Los Angeles Police Department tampering with evidence testimony.

Nicole Simpson was raised to martyrdom as the symbol of spousal abuse, led by white women's rights advocates. Old and newer sources marketed every aspect they could dredge up for sale. So far there are no reliable published reports of the millions made off of Simpson and the media created "Trial of the Century." However, over ninety books have been published and over one million references have been made on the internet.

Simpson was found liable for the murders of Nicole and Ron Goldman. The plaintiffs were awarded 8.5 million dollars. Mark Fuhrman, charged with perjury in the criminal trial got a slap on the wrist before the Simpson civil trial: a three hundred dollar fine and three years probation.

After the bad taste blow-out party for O.J. the day of his aquittal, he continued to be publically arrogant and insensitive to how much he was hated and the possible impact his egotistical behavior had on the upcoming civil trial. He mugged for cameras, made wise cracks, became a golf course bum, called into talk shows uninvited and was generally obnoxious in public, still putting on a front for the public. Unfortunately for the African American community Simpson is viewed by a large number of whites as a "black man" first, symbolic of black men. He is also linked to the negative stereotypes of black men through the ages. In fact he is seen as worse than average, as mentioned, because he was an acclaimed national hero to whites. Nevertheless, he is certainly not in the league with genuine African American male sports heroes.

Jackie Robinson

He became a legend playing for the Brooklyn Dodgers. But, he also suffered all the indignities that could be heaped upon a man because Jackie Robinson embodied the Four Fears of white men—intelligence, strength, sexuality and anger. One could say that Jackie Robinson gave up his life to integrate baseball. He died at age fifty-two, diagnosed as a victim of diabetes, but the inhuman demands placed upon him as the first mainstream African American baseball player no doubt also contributed to his death.

The burden that prominent African men bear is a load that forces them to represent the entire race as they try to do whatever job they are called upon to do. The positions they occupy also carry with them the load of being a model or spokesman for all African Americans. That they die younger and wear out sooner, prominent or not, is reflected in the statistics. Baseball champion Jackie Robinson gave his life to become the first African American to play in the white major leagues. His superhuman performance included not only his great skills in sports, but he was subjected to the worst treatment imaginable from white bigots, racists—prejudiced cowards. Nor did it end with Robinson. Other African American baseball players were attacked, especially Hank Aaron as he approached exceeding Babe Ruth's home run record.

Jackie Robinson was one of five children who had brothers who were outstanding athletes like himself. However, Robinson was one of the most accomplished all-around athletes this nation has ever produced.[46] Before he turned twenty he was outstanding in basketball, baseball, football and broke the broad jump record in 1938. Duke Snider, later a Brooklyn Dodger team mate, said he saw Jackie in junior college leave in the middle of a baseball game to compete in the broad jump. Then he would go back and finish the baseball game.

Robinson was so good the director of athletics at UCLA said he was afraid the four coaches would fight among themselves to try to win Robinson over. Robinson was so special that recruiters were willing to pay his tuition out of state to keep him from their competing schools.[47]

He is still considered the greatest open field runner in the 1990's, said childhood friend Ray Bartlett.[48] Stanford coach Tiny Thornbull said Robinson was the greatest backfield runner he had seen in twenty-five years.[49] If he had not played football he would have been one of the greatest basketball players of all time, said one coach. These accolades are reminders when mentioning Robinson's fantastic baseball career.

He was just twenty years old when he completed his outstanding, brilliant year at UCLA, but at that earlier stage of his career, he had already experienced the daggers and cannon balls thrown at him for being a black youth in America. He had been witness to a cross burning on the lawn of his home and jeered and taunted by white gangs as he and his brother went to and from school.

But Jackie was in no way a wimp. He was high spirited and confrontative. It is reported that sometimes he had scrapes with the law. However, the black community knows that good or bad, a black youth is subject to have scrapes with the law anywhere in America because they are likely to be set up, framed and or harassed. He faced the cold fact of racism in the military when he was court-martialed for refusing the orders of a white bus driver to move. Added insults occurred when the government subjected him to harsh, degrading experiences as an officer in an all black Army unit.

Robinson learned early of the necessity to protect himself from white men's fears of black male sexuality. He told Carl Rowan, journalist, he was wary of white women who fawned over him in college where he was big man on campus.[50] He seemed standoffish and arrogant, but he was shy, not from inexperience, but from mistrust. He said he remembered how Pasadena authorities used white girls to tempt black employees who joined in efforts to desegregate swimming pools; then they were accused of making insulting passes at the white girls and fired.[51]

Like Paul Robeson, Muhammad Ali and Joe Louis, the medical records do not reveal the real causes of illness or death, but their historical records make it crystal clear that racism, white supremacy, bigotry, and prejudice were major contributing factors. The toll for Jackie Robinson was internalizing his rage for three years after joining the Dodgers. However, all Robinson had faced from racists before that time was ingrained in his body, including an old neglected sports injury that plagued him through his career.

Robinson had to agree to take, without a whimper, whatever indignity was thrown at him for the first three years that he played for the Dodgers. Imagine the effect it had on his physical condition. It is not surprising that he was diagnosed with diabetes, a malfunction of the pancreas, one of the major regulators of the human body.

The white racist sports writers aided and abetted the strife Robinson faced from the racist baseball fans. Overall, baseball has been slow to integrate across the board. Furthermore, it was unrealistic to expect that accepting one African American in baseball was the forerunner of a renaissance in racial injustice in America. Nevertheless, the black players in the major leagues owe it all to Jackie Robinson. For a brief time he held the spotlight as a harbinger of social change, but it "grounded out."

"Jackie Robinson was not simply carrying the whole race on his shoulders...he was driving the consciousness of black capacities more deeply into American culture than any black person had ever done previously...If he had done nothing else in his life after 1947, he would be entitled to be an American legend, but he went on and had a very distinguished career."[52]

Faulkner aptly tallies what Robinson faced with the Brooklyn Dodgers and in the training camps. In every town he was put in segregated housing, and what was worse, his teammates barely spoke to him in the clubhouse and ignored him in the field.

In all the cities he was showered with racial slurs, including being called a "nigger pussy" in Syracuse, New York. In Baltimore, rioting and bloodshed were ever-present threats. The Pittsburgh Pirates refused to take the field until they were told they would have to forfeit the game. Radio mics on the field had to be replaced due to the vile language hurled at Robinson by the Pirates. The Saint Louis Cardinals allegedly tried to initiate a strike against Robinson; the Chicago Cubs also took a unanimous strike vote against him; however, they backed off when the league office said any striker would be disbarred for life. Nevertheless, the Cubs' starring pitchers had standing orders to knock Robinson down. He was knocked down repeatedly and no one, not one official or anyone else objected, not even Robinson. Cubs coach, Roy Johnson, accused Branch Rickey, his manager, of covering up a rape of a white girl by Robinson during college.

In Cincinnati, the taunts came from the dugout, as well as the stands, " '…you nigger son of a bitch, you shoeshine boy', and all the rest."[53] Some of the hate was serious enough to warrant the FBI searching roof tops and buildings before games. Mail poured into the Dodgers with death and kidnapping threats against Robinson, his wife and baby.

The wort attacks came in Philadelphia. An Alabama redneck, Ben Chapman, was well known for his racism and he led his team, the Philadelphia Phillies, in "…unprintable barrage of verbal abuse against Robinson that lasted throughout the series." Richie Ashburn, a Phillies' player, admitted to and apologized years later for tossing a black cat out on the playing field at Jackie.

Robinson reported, "…Almost as if it had been synchronized by some master conductor, hate poured fourth from the Phillies' dugout. 'Hey Nigger…go back to the cotton field; They are waiting for you in the jungles black boy; hey snowflake, which one of these white boy's wives are you dating tonight?'"[54] (They expressed the ever-present sexual fear of white men.) The Phillies waved, hooted, and made obscene gestures at Robinson. They warned Robinson's team they would catch diseases from him.

The moth-eaten Benjamin Franklin Hotel in Philadelphia put Robinson's baggage out on the sidewalk! He was refused housing in most cities.

Despite all this torment, Robinson was hitting and smashing records, making the Four Fears even more ominous to the cowardly white males.

After an unbelievable stellar career, where Robinson kept his head and upheld the race, he finally fell victim to the government's use of African American athletes for political and propaganda reasons. As they had done with Jesse Owens, the great track star, who later became a puppet against the civil rights movement, Muhammad Ali who was indicted for draft dodging, Joe Louis, who voluntarily entertained troops during World War II, but they got him for taxes afterwards. Robinson was convinced to testify before the House un-American Activities Committee against Paul Robeson. It was orchestrated by the government forces to destroy Paul Robeson. The scenario is always the same, put a black man or black people to take positions opposite each other.

Robinson's testimony before HUAC, was reported worldwide. His vilification of Robeson as a traitor and communist was because Robinson's own group, "Negro and Allied Veterans," was accused of being a communist front.[55] To remove the stigma, it is reported that Robinson agreed to testify. Robinson was the most honored and respected African American. They had him to discredit Robeson because Robeson was the most respected African American around the world at that time.

The Four Fears of white men and the concomitant guilt was whipped into a fury of witch hunts that was driven to falsely accuse Paul Robeson. He spoke out around the world against injustice and accused the U.S. before the United Nations.

7
Intellectuals, Politicians, Activist Heroes

Marcus Garvey

Marcus Manasseh Garvey was born in Jamaica, in 1887, of parents descended from unmixed African stock, the Maroons, escaped African warriors.[1] The Maroons are held in high esteem because they fought for their independence and obtained a treaty, a rarity, with the British in 1793. Garvey grew up under that proud heritage, also influenced by the strength and strong will of his father who loved reading, and the gentle forgiving persona of his mother. His early education in Catholic schools brought affiliation with whites and white students until the age when white youth usually start to disassociate themselves from their black classmates. In his autobiography Garvey emphasized that although beating students was de rigueur of the day, he refused to submit to whippings by his teachers because of his inherent disdain for humiliation and defeat. Later on these characteristics and his upbringing were the basis of his great pride, courage and leadership.

Garvey's early travels enlightened him and exposed him to racial prejudice. These experiences, reading about the harsh conditions of African Americans and studying the works of African scholar, Duse Mohammed Ali, helped him to develop his race consciousness and his quest of Africa for Africans. He was also influenced by Booker T. Washington's autobiography, *Up From Slavery*. Garvey greatly admired Washington and wrote to him toward the end of his life.[2] Washington invited Garvey to the United States to meet with him, but Washington died in 1916 before they actually met. Nevertheless, the Garvey Movement became the greatest of its kind in history. Because of Garvey's uncanny brilliance, the preeminent elder historian, John Henrik Clarke, reports that Marcus Garvey is one of the most written about Africans. Clark said he became an academic industry.

The Four Fears were germane factors to the unprecedented attack on Garvey by world governments and powers. The most frightening aspect of Marcus Garvey's movement was his intelligence and organizational ability, and his mental and physical strength; due to his knowledge of the legacy of suffering of people of color under white supremacy, anger was also a motivation for Garvey's zealous leadership. Although he was not noted for his physical prowess, because it is inherent in the white male's overall fear of black men, the mere fact that he was a black man made him a sexual threat.

Garvey saw the need for race leadership. His inheritance, experience, intellect, and spiritual strength enabled him to develop a unique organization of African Americans never before, or since, seen in the United States. However, the primary goals of the UNIA, the Universal Negro Improvement Association, were the most audacious. Garvey had in his sights the intention to redeem the African continent for Africans in Africa and in the diaspora—the United States, South America, the Caribbean, etc.

Garvey became the greatest threat of his time to European interests in Africa. After World War I, the Western Powers were committed to hacking up Africa amongst themselves and mentally and physically enslaving the entire continent in order to purloin the natural and human resources. In wake of their intentions, Garvey planned a super government controlled by black people under one discipline, similar to the Catholic Church. He appealed to race patriotism, Africans spirited to these shores from the start had dreamed, plotted, planned and acted to redress their enslavement. Although Garvey's Back-To-Africa Movement was not seminal, it came at a time when the climate was rife with dissatisfaction over white supremacy, the newer subservient role for Africans in America and the Caribbean after World War I.

In the United States, Garvey attracted thousands of people and millions of dollars for his movement; vast numbers were West Indians. Using his flair for promotion he organized an army in uniforms, The African Legion, as well as the Black Cross Nurses, choral groups, and high-spirited juvenile auxiliaries. His organization bought an auditorium seating 6000, Liberty Hall. He was a master orator with a penchant for drama. He and his "Court of Ethiopia" paced the auditorium. The crowds rallied to their anthem "Ethiopia, Thou Land of our Fathers." They heard Garvey boast of his proud African heritage and his jet black skin. He gave fiery speeches, he promoted military might by parading uniformed men, soldiers of "The great Army of Africa." His Africa Motor Corps had young black males as the UNIA's standard bearers. Marchers paraded with signs and pictures of a black Madonna and child as well as heroes like Frederick Douglass and others. Their posters read "Free Africa," "Princes Shall Come Out of Egypt," "The Negro Will Build Cruisers and Submarines," and "African Scientists Will Win the War." Standard bearing colors were red, black, green and the motto is "One God! One Aim! One Destiny!"

Garvey was a messiah to African Americans but a foreboding entity to governments and others with vested interests. By 1920, he had launched The Negro Factories Corporation and had a chain of cooperative grocery stores, a restaurant, a steam laundry, tailor and dress-making shop, millinery store and publishing house. His aim was to erect and manage factories in the large manufacturing areas of the United States, Central America and the West Indies. Black people were primed to support his enterprises to secure employment for Africans of color. Garvey's astute understanding of his race led him to believe the best approach to gain support of the masses was to appeal to their universal need for security. Economic security was a vehicle toward establishment of nationhood in the Back-To-Africa Movement.

As stated before, Garvey came into power at a time of great disillusionment among African Americans after the First World War.

Hopes were crushed by rampant national racism, riots against black people and mistreatment of black veterans. Lured to the North by white industrialists to work and cut out immigrant labor, many black people now found themselves subject to many of the conditions from which they had fled in the notorious South. These factories were a ready ground for Garvey, dubbed the "Black Moses," to take hold.

His great insight led him to publish his own newspaper, the militant and highly influential *Negro World*. In his youth Garvey had learned the printing trade and he said of himself that due to his intelligence and strong manly character, he was able to become a manager of a print shop and director of the men at the early age of eighteen.

The black press crusaded for justice as the most respected instrument of information and advocacy during that time. It was a free press because it was not controlled by advertisers, politicians, other ethnic and religious groups as many black publications are today as a result of the "Integration Movement."

Further evidence of Garvey's greatness and threat to certain elements was his organization of the Black Star Steamship Corp. Under black control, he planned to increase trade between the United States, the West Indies and Africa and to carry African Americans home to Africa.

Garvey's vision for Africa was a threat to white supremacy in the U.S. He believed the movement would redeem African Americans, give them hope, power and self determination. However, at the time black people were still needed for semi-slave labor in the United States and to continue to serve the fantasy of white supremacist superiority. Furthermore, the movement would impact the economy because Garvey was encouraging African Americans to invest in their own economic development. His brochure said, "Write the name of the race across commercial history of the world."[3] Garvey hoped that his objective to take back the continent of Africa would inspire African Americans to be moved to action.

Attacks by European-Western powers, betrayals by blacks and whites, poor planning, implementation and some apparent personal failings, led to the dissolution of the UNIA and Garvey being railroaded into prison. He suffered the fate of most African and African American leaders of principle and ability. The betrayal by Liberian leaders with whom Garvey had negotiated the return to Africa settlement is blamed among others on W.E.B. DuBois, a founder of the NAACP. However, Clarke points out that DuBois' power was limited and the actual reason for the withdrawal of the Liberian sanctuary offer was due to Liberian internal conflicts.[4] The conflicts ensued because Liberia was not truly an independent African state, and when the outside influences pressured them they were forced to renege on their commitment.

To cut off the head of the movement with international implications, Garvey was indicted and imprisoned for mail fraud in the United States. Yet his movement, his strength, intelligence and courage lives on in the heart of every movement and attempt to liberate Africans and African Americans. His initiation of the UNIA goals and principles and his leadership of 6,000,000 members has not been matched as we head toward the twenty-first century. Nor has the Four Fears of white men been abated largely because black people have been influenced by the life and vision of Marcus Garvey to continue to struggle for liberation, economic and social justice.

Garvey said in a speech before his imprisonment in 1923:

> "...Marcus Garvey has entered the fight for redemption of a country. From the graves of millions of my forebearers at this hour I hear the cry, and I am going to answer it even though hell is cut loose before Marcus Garvey. From the silence make for their memory, this fight that shall leave a glaring page in the history of man.
>
> I did not bring myself here; they brought me from my silent repose in Africa 300 years ago, and this is only the first Marcus Garvey. They have thought that they could for 300 years brutalize a race. They have thought that they could for 300 years steep a soul of a race in blood and darkness and let it go at that. They make a terrible mistake...."

97

I repeat if they think they can stamp out the souls of 400,000,000 black men, they make a tremendous and terrible mistake. We are no longer dogs; we are no longer peons; we are no longer serfs—we are men....[5]

W.E.B. DuBois

There is no presumption to attempt to discuss in this short space the brilliant record of the life of Dr. W.E.B. DuBois. The purpose is to disclose some of the incidents he endured at the hands of his enemies because he was an African American man committed to the liberation of his people and world justice, especially those people suffering under white supremacy.

W.E.B. DuBois, the greatest sociologist and scholar of his time, was a warrior for his race, first and foremost, and a fighter for world peace. Dr. DuBois was in the category of intelligence that put him on the African American men's endangered list. He started early in his life to work, study, campaign, speak, and travel around the world for justice. In the midst of the harsh times for the average black person, he was born in 1868 in Massachusetts in comfortable circumstances to a loving family. He died ninety-three years later in Accra, Ghana in self imposed exile.

After his years of honorable endeavors in many areas, he was arrested in the U.S. at age eighty, charged as an alleged communist sympathizer because of his membership in the Peace Information Center, despite the fact he had resigned prior to the indictment. Like Paul Robeson, he was snared in the anti-Communist witch hunt hysteria of the McCarthy era, but for these giants it was a continuation of the country's reaction to black men since slavery. Dr. DuBois earned a stellar, international reputation as a warrior for peace. He was humiliated before the world simply because of his life-long quest to make the world a better place and to influence the United States to live up to the Constitution and the Bill of Rights.

One of the founders of the National Association for the Advancement of Colored People, he earned a Ph.D. from Harvard after completing Fisk University where he was inspired by his excellent teachers and motivated to start his life-long pursuit of freedom and progress among Negroes. His exposure to Fisk had been enlightening and although he was aloof and engrossed in scholarship, he said he was heartened to be in the warm atmosphere with his racial contemporaries. His doctoral thesis at Harvard University, "Suppression of the Slave Trade," and his research led to his election to the American Historical Society. Because he was extremely gifted, he was afforded the opportunity to travel and study in Europe where he was spared the racial prejudice and bigotry he faced at Harvard and throughout the U.S.

Dr. DuBois was a man who was proud of his African ancestry; he became acutely aware of the state of black people in the U.S., but he strove to never let the prejudice and bigotry interfere in his determination to learn and to work for his people's self determination, liberation and continued scholarship.

Because of a wealthy white woman, Susan P. Wharton's interest in the city's Seventh Ward in Philadelphia where rich and poor, black and white lived, in 1896, Dr. DuBois was given a special invitation to conduct a study for the University of Pennsylvania. Wharton prevailed upon the Provost to study the condition of black people in the city's Seventh Ward.

Philadelphia, which had and still has one of the worst reputations for racism, has also produced some of the most noted African American leaders in the history of the U.S. Some of the leadership of that time was due to the aid of people like Susan Wharton and Samuel McCune Lindsay, a member of the Sociology Department of the Wharton School, who obtained DuBois for the position.

Nevertheless, DuBois reported that the position was in some ways dehumanizing as he was singled out and treated differently from other professors. Dr. DuBois said:

> There must have been some opposition for the invitation was not particularly cordial. I was offered a salary of $800 for a limited period of one year. I was given no real academic standing, no office at the University, no official recognition of any kind; my name was even eventually omitted from the catalogue; I had no contact with students, and very little with members of the faculty, even in my department. With my bride of three months, I settled in one room over a cafeteria run by a College Settlement in the worst part of the Seventh Ward. We lived there a year, in the midst of an atmosphere of dirt, drunkenness, poverty and crime. Murder sat on our doorsteps, police were our government and philanthropy dropped in with periodic advice.[6]

Despite these slights, Dr. DuBois diligently completed the landmark study, still referred to by scholars nearly one hundred years later: *The Philadelphia Negro: A Social Study.*

Dr. DuBois said he conducted the study because he wanted "to free his race through history and social science by means of research and writing."[7] His objective in the Philadelphia study was to research and collect data through scientific methods to affect the ignorance whites had about blacks. His research, unfortunately, did not receive the attention he hoped for. In fact, it was unavailable for over fifty years, reissued in 1967, by Dr. Digby Baltzell, University of Pennsylvania. Dr. DuBois never received the money he deserved for his book and his research. However, Baltzell who did profit from the reissue, upheld white supremacy by stating in the introduction to the republication that Dr. DuBois lied when he said he was mistreated by the University of Pennsylvania. Baltzell said that the minutes of the University's Board of Trustees did not disclose any opposition to DuBois' appointment.

Really. Although the opposition may not have been in the minutes, the circumstances as reported by Dr. DuBois speak for themselves.

Using his mighty pen and his scholarship, Dr. DuBois edited the NAACP publication, *The Crisis*, for many years to help rally for the causes of African American people. The publication was very influential and southern congressmen ordered it stricken from the mails. Asked by the NAACP to investigate treatment of black soldiers during the First World War, Dr. DuBois went to Europe and unearthed a communiqué by the French military ordering French soldiers not to be friendly with black soldiers. DuBois created a sensation when he printed the directive in *The Crisis*. Tirelessly working in the NAACP, writing and publishing *The Crisis*, this slightly built man, educated in black and white schools, used the methodologies he learned to wage his battle.

Immediately after the First World War in which black men fought and died to defend the U.S. and Europe, they and other black people were subjected to some of the worse race riots in U.S. history. The Klan was night riding and lynching black men, burning crosses and terrorizing the country. African Americans were being accosted and set upon on the streets and railways and even attacked in their homes, north and south. Instead of the government cracking down on the white perpetrators of these vicious crimes, after 1919 it started to harass labor groups and investigate black publications to charge them with sedition and radicalism. The government went so far as to raid the NAACP offices and confront Dr. DuBois.

Nevertheless, Dr. DuBois led the way in including Africa in the struggle for people of color; he was seriously opposed by the U.S. and international colonial forces. He organized the Pan-African Congress to free Africa from colonial rule. It was censored by the white press in the U.S., but he began to be a severe threat to white supremacy, in race, politics and economic issues.

Dr. DuBois recognized the futility of continuing to support and participate in politics after the treachery of Woodrow Wilson who promised African Americans freedom before his election, but when elected he initiated harsh segregation laws in the federal government, and he was closed mouthed about the reign of terror and lynchings in the country. Eventually, Dr. DuBois averred Socialism. This move labeled him as a dangerous Communist and a potent threat to the U.S. Nevertheless, Dr. DuBois pursued his convictions and his dream of equality on every critical level for all.

Notwithstanding his dedication to his people, Dr. DuBois, who could have gone any way he chose, was enmeshed in the debate over the better way for African Americans to obtain their liberation. At one time or another he was at odds with Marcus Garvey and "the Back to Africa Movement," Booker T. Washington and his accommodationist philosophy, or A. Philip Randolph, Head of the Pullman Porters Union, a "young turk," who believed Dr. DuBois was too old to lead. Dr. DuBois even found himself at odds with the Board of Directors of the NAACP for his stands, and eventually he resigned from The Crisis due to the NAACP's Board of Director's fear of the U.S. government.

The resignation came in the wake of the atrocity of thirteen black soldiers being hanged in 1918. The black men were serving the United States citizens, yet they were hanged because, allegedly, they were involved in a race riot in Houston, Texas. DuBois condemned the legal lynching of black servicemen in The Crisis. The Justice Department threatened the NAACP with "harming the war effort."[8] The board reacted by making Dr. DuBois clear everything in *The Crisis* first with their legal consultant. This was faintly disguised censorship and a slap in Dr. DuBois' face after the great dedication he gave to the NAACP and *The Crisis*. It also showed great disrespect for a man of Dr. DuBois' brilliance, academic and political astuteness.

Decade after decade for seventy years until he died at age ninety-three on the eve of the March on Washington in 1963, Dr. DuBois was the champion for freedom and justice like no man before or since his time. His life's record includes the highest achievements, including authoring numerous books and articles besides *The Crisis*. Some people were put off by his aloofness and his admittedly sharp tongue. These were minor flaws overshadowed by his great mind, morality, sensibilities and commitment to his race.

For all his efforts, he found himself at age seventy-six, poor and unemployed, having accumulated no wealth. Worse than that, at age eighty he was indicted, handcuffed before the public and humiliated by his government for his affiliation with the Peace Information Center. Over 5,000,000 students in seventy-one countries registered indignation with the U.S. government for persecuting Dr. DuBois. To defend the case he needed $100,000, therefore, at his advanced age he was compelled to travel around the U.S. and beg for money for his defense. Eventually, the trumped up charges did not hold up in court and he was freed. However, Dr. DuBois' travail was not over because he had been indicted in the era of anti-Communism fervor. He was still marked and shunned. Courageous to the end, Dr. DuBois wrote "In Battle for Peace," the story of his indictment and trial to exonerate himself. Whispered tales implied he was really guilty but the government was soft on him because of his age. Even many black brothers and sisters avoided him just as they did Paul Robeson. (This author can testify to the fact that Dr. DuBois' books were removed from bookstores, verified by an antiquarian in 1966.) Through it all he kept on working, he did not hide or avoid the public that deserted him in his time of trouble. His belief in the Talented Tenth, intellectuals and scholars to teach and help the less fortunate, was seriously eroded after his indictment. The Talented Tenth never came to his aid when he needed them, much less their down trodden countrymen. Dr. DuBois learned at a critical time, that lacking cultural awareness, once educated and indoctrinated in the U.S. system, unless systematically deprogrammed, the talented and the untalented react the way they are trained to react by their masters.[9]

Dr. DuBois was a strong African American man, superior to all of his white contemporaries in the genre of the intelligent black men whom whites fear and therefore try to destroy. He was the apotheosis of the intelligence and strength in African American men that strikes terror and fear in the heart of white supremacists. They made every effort to destroy him, but he died in his ancestral home, Ghana, in honor, embued with the love and adoration he earned and richly deserved, but never got in his homeland—but happy and free.

Paul Robeson

All four aspects of the dominant fears of intelligence, strength, sexuality and anger were exuded by Paul Robeson. Brilliant, Phi Beta Kappa, and a football star at Rutgers University, twice All American; he also earned a degree from Columbia University Law School. Robeson possessed a magnificent singing voice, was an astute actor, had a winning charm and a strong, beautiful physique.

Totally fearless before the forces of evil stacked against his people and disenfranchised others, he dared to speak out in righteous anger, putting his own life in jeopardy.

He died in Philadelphia, Pennsylvania, in 1976, after spending his life working and speaking out against injustice around the world. At home in the U.S., in 1930, unvarnished evidence of racial fears and jealousy were let loose in a barrage of protests when a larger than life bronze nude statue of Robeson, entitled "Negro Spiritual," by Antonio Salemme was presented to the Philadelphia Art Alliance. The very sight of a gorgeous, nude, intellectual, African American man, raised such great furor that Salemme was told that the "colored problem" seemed to be unusually great in Philadelphia. But it was not the "colored problem" it was the white problem. The sculpture was boxed up and returned to Salemme. Nor was the City of Brotherly Love supportive of him during his trying days to come when the government attacked him. However, near the end of his life the African American community did rally around him.

Paul Robeson, who became an international African American hero, was a descendent of a noble family. His father, a Presbyterian minister who had escaped from slavery by way of the Underground Railroad, later worked his way through Lincoln University in Pennsylvania. He was a role model for little Paul who worshiped him. Rev. W.D. Robeson married a Philadelphia school teacher, Maria Louisa Bustill. She was from a brilliant family whose family tree included many teachers, artists and scholars including the world renowned artist, Henry Ossowa Tanner and Dr. Nathan Mossell the first African American physician to graduate from the University of Pennsylvania. Robeson's great grandfather was Cyrus Bustill, who baked bread for George Washington's troops. In 1787, Bustill founded the Free African Society, the first mutual aid organization for African Americans located in Philadelphia. Also, the Bustills took part in operating the Underground Railroad which helped scores to escape bondage like Robeson's father. Bustleton, Pennsylvania, was named after Cyrus Bustill. Robersonville, North Carolina, was named for the Robeson slave holders. One of the earliest slave petitions on record, by Ned Griffin, 1784, urged the government to grant him the denied freedom promised him after he served in the Revolutionary War. The petition was denied him by his owner an Abner Roberson! (Over time the "r" was dropped from the name.)

Paul Robeson grew in the knowledge of his esteemed heritage through the teachings of his loving parents. That heritage, his intelligence, and his equally brilliant and faithful wife, Eslanda Robeson, helped to sustain his courage when the government tried to destroy him when he spoke out for freedom and justice. In addition, much of the black community disowned him at that time.

"Loyalty to Convictions," a speech that the government used against him to try to prove he was a Communist, was chosen, Robeson said, because it was "the text of my father's life."[10] Loyalty to his convictions was Robeson's unwavering motto throughout his life as he strove to obtain rights, primarily for African Americans but for all people as stated before.

Certainly the Bustill's, Robeson's illustrious history in the development of the U.S. predates the Americans who attempted to destroy Robeson in the name of preserving the country from the "Red Menace." A black man's history and character are rarely respected. In his book *Here I Stand*, Robeson said that he sadly saw his older brother fall to the systematic injustices to which millions of black men have succumbed.

> Reed [his brother] is dead now. He won no honors in the classroom, pulpit or platform. Yet, I remember him with love. Restless, rebellious, scoffing at conventions, defiant of the white man's law—I've known many Negroes like Reed. I see them every day. Blindly, in their own reckless manner, they seek a way out for themselves; alone they pound their fists and fury against walls that only the shoulder of many can topple. 'Don't ever take low,' was the lesson Reed taught me. 'Stand up to them and hit back harder than they hit you!' When the many have learned that lesson, everything will be different and then the fiery ones like Reed will be able to live out their lives in peace and no one will have cause to frown on them.[11]

Reed rejected his father's way to defeat white oppression. Paul, on the other hand, never considered opposing his father. He said his love for learning and a constant search for truth was welcomed from his father.

Paul's father had a deep sonorous basso voice and singing at home was a regular activity. When it was discovered that Paul had a good voice too, he joined the church choir, sang in the glee club and started to sing for entertainment. This was the beginning of what was to be his primary occupation in years to come. He, however, went way beyond merely singing songs. In song, he sang out for freedom and carried the message wherever he went. When he was denied permission to travel, he was already trained in the classics and ballads, he spent his time in the government imposed exile in his own country researching and learning folk songs of people from around the world.

Robeson was born April 8, 1898, and he grew up in the racist Jim Crow town of Princeton, New Jersey. "Under the caste system in Princeton, the Negro, restricted in menial jobs at low pay and lacking any semblance of political rights or bargaining power, could not hope for justice..." said Robeson.[12] Despite the outside environment, his home and the African American community were the staples in his life. His mother, a teacher, died early in his life; he was only seven, nevertheless, she left an indelible impression on him. She was of mixed African, Indian and white Quaker stock, said Robeson. His brother Rev. Benjamin Robeson, in an appendix to *Here I Stand* said their mother was "a queen in the realm of education which carried all of its power into the spiritual realm. Despite suffering from failing eyesight, she wrote as many of her husband's sermons as he did," said Benjamin.[13]

Paul was exposed to the classic debates of the time between Booker T. Washington and W.E.B. DuBois which were largely centered on educational goals for black people. Washington advocated manual training while DuBois advocated that all learning must be for black people. Rev. Robeson's philosophy concurred with DuBois, thus Paul had eight years of Latin in high school and college, four years of Greek and the well known European classics of the day, Virgil and Homer. (Years later Robeson and DuBois would be caught in the same government witch hunt. Two of the most brilliant men in history were publicly scorned, vilified and, in Robeson's case, nearly murdered in an attempt to destroy him.)

At home, Paul's father taught him public speaking and oration, and his successful days as class orator and debater were learned under the skill and loving guidance of his father. "...His love for the eloquent and meaningful word and his insistence on purity of diction made their impress," said Robeson.[14]

Although his education was Eurocentric, Robeson did not shun his African heritage. In 1915, in an oratorical contest at his high school, he won third place reciting Wendell Phillips' famous speech of Toussaint L'Ouverture on white supremacy.

Remarkably, he won a scholarship to Rutgers in an examination that covered four years of course work in the same three hour period in which others only had to know their senior course work. He had not known about the preliminary test the other students took the previous year that absolved them from taking the four year exam.

From an early age Robeson said he learned what every black person, especially black men, in America lives with:

> I had come to accept and follow a certain protective tactic of Negro life in America, and I did not fully break the pattern until many years later. Even while demonstrating that he is really an equal (and, strangely the proof must be superior performance!), the Negro must never appear to be challenging white superiority. Climb up if you can—but don't act 'uppity'. Always show that you are grateful. (Even if what you have gained has been wrested from unwilling powers, be sure to be grateful lest they take it all away.) Above all, do nothing to give them cause to fear you, for then the oppressing hand, which might at times ease up a little, will surely become a fist to knock you down again![15]

His fingernails were torn from his hand during a play when his own foot ball team mates spiked him. Despite this malicious attack Robeson excelled in football as mentioned before. After working his way through law school at Columbia University, where he was exposed to more racism, his artistic talent as an actor led him to Hollywood and a career on stage. Unlike those black clowns, buffoons and detractors of the race on television, video and stage in this era, Robeson, after making a few movies, decided that he had an obligation to present a dignified, intelligent image of black people to the public. He said, "...I came to understand that the Negro artist could not view the matter simply in terms of his individual interests, and that he had a responsibility to his people...."[16] His acting included his famous role in Shakespeare's *Othello* as well as films. His vocal career was equally as eminent.

Secure in his racial heritage and loyalty to it, well educated and sensitive, he traveled around the world and was exposed to other injustices in other nations. These exposures compounded his outrage at the injustices his people were suffering at home. He became an outspoken activist for freedom; this led to unprecedented actions taken against him by the U.S. government and probably contributed to the long siege of illness that ended his life. The State Department rescinded his passport because he went around the world singing and advocating for human rights. In *Here I Stand* he said, "...I have suffered by being denied a passport....while no one has charged that I have broken any law, I have been forced to suffer the loss of many thousands of dollars in fees offered to me as an artist...and the legal expense of fighting my case for the past seven years has been considerable."[17]

On top of this, Robeson brought down the power of all the colonial governments on his head when he not only fought against white supremacy in the U.S., but he spoke out against it in the colonialism under Britain, France and other countries as well as the horrendous system of apartheid in South Africa. The colonial powers joined in a conspiracy with the U.S. to silence Robeson.

It is speculated that an attempt was made on Robeson's life by agents of some government because his international influence and respect for his beliefs were a threat to Western domination of people of color and the Cold War between the Western powers Russia and China. Several Robeson biographers report that he became mysteriously ill after attending a social function. This illness was the forerunner of the subsequent sickness that eventually took his life.

It was during the period of red baiting and fear of Communist Russia and China that the destructive acts increased. Today, Russia and her former allies, including China, are in bed with or business partners with the United States while African Americans and people of color around the globe are still seeking the justice and liberty for which Robeson fought. Yet, Robeson and many other activists and artists, black and white, were hounded, jailed, dishonored, or assassinated to obliterate the alleged Communist threat.

In 1951, Paul Robeson in an historic and courageous act, led a delegation to the United Nations and presented a petition charging the United States with genocide. In "We Charge Genocide," William L. Patterson says, "...even a cursory examination would reveal the savage racist policy..."[18] Robeson took up the struggle of fallen hero Marcus Garvey and joined the heroic, international struggles for freedom and rights waged by W.E.B. DuBois. The United States government severely punished all three for their valiant acts to awaken and save their people.

Senator Joseph McCarthy misused his position in congress to take away work and intimidate citizens in a witch hunt. At the same time, the former chief of the FBI, J. Edgar Hoover, ran his nefarious shadow and spy government. He posed as the consummate bachelor sacrificing a spotless personal life to devote himself to defending his country from crime and criminals. Meanwhile, Hoover led a double life shielded from the public by the media until after he died. As the self-proclaimed top cop and guardian of moral standards, Hoover harassed Robeson and later exposed Martin Luther King's alleged dalliances. Hoover's secret life as a cross-dresser and consorter with mobsters was kept hidden. McCarthy and Hoover led the campaigns to destroy black heroes who were pilloried as were Martin Luther King and Malcolm X in the next generation.

After all he had suffered and sacrificed for the peoples of the world, finally, Robeson was buoyed by the civil rights movement led by African American youth. He wrote in *Here I Stand*:

> ...I smile to see in these newspapers' photographs the faces, so bright, so solemn of our young heroes—the children of Little Rock....And to the list could be added the names of all the other Negro children in the Southland who have given us great new epics of courage and dignity. The patter of their feet as they walk through Jim Crow barriers to attend school

in the thunder of the marching men of Joshua and the world rocks beneath their tread.[19]

What Robeson said, what he did, the sacrifices he and his family made for freedom, live on and are more encouraging now than ever. Heroes like Robeson are icons and beacons of hope to the masses of people, although they are not under the overt lash of the slave masters, they are still the slaves of the economic and political conditions that persist. Despite the violation of his rights and unfairness visited on him, Paul Robeson's strength, moral fiber, intelligence, and dedication are legacies that will endure when the world's charlatans and despots are ground into dust under the heels of humanity and the wheels of precious freedom.

Adam Clayton Powell

Debasing African American men reaches into all areas of society. It is fomented and nurtured in places like the United States Congress, colleges, universities, institutes, think tanks, and businesses; it knows no boundaries. Therefore, being elected to the United States Congress is no safe haven for black men. Duly elected to represent their constituencies, nevertheless, they have been drummed out of Congress on trumped up charges, lies, half truths and manipulations. Possibly the most concentrated, underhanded efforts were exerted against Adam Clayton Powell, Jr., an African American man ever faithful to—black and poor people, labor, education and his brand of religion. He was the white man's nemesis: intelligent in the extreme, handsome, attractive to women and angry. Although he looked like one of them, he preferred to be recognized as a militant black man.

Powell was flamboyant, in the genre of the brilliant, charismatic criminal attorney Cecil B. Moore who revolutionized Philadelphia in the same era. Powell was also a deft, confident, charismatic minister from Harlem, New York. He reached political heights in Harlem and amassed an unprecedented legislative record in Congress before the powerful forces that guard the gates of white supremacy destroyed him. Powell's destruction was a well orchestrated plot that took years to ferment, and he was voted out of Congress in the early 1970s.

The well known historical conspiracy to oppress and demoralize black men with new inroads were implemented against Powell. He was able to stave off efforts to embarrass, intimidate and defile him until a black woman was used to file charges in court against him. The book jacket to his autobiography, *Adam by Adam*, states, "Flamboyant Adam Clayton Powell, as chairman of the powerful House, Education and Labor Committee, probably wielded more political clout than any other black man in this nation's history."[20]

By his style and his demeanor, he was put in the "Bad Nigger" category of forty years earlier. But this time it wasn't Jack Johnson, an uneducated boxer, it was Adam Clayton Powell, a well educated black man, handsome by white standards, but like Johnson, fearless and threatening to whites.

Powell was the son of a prominent minister, who pastored the largest African American congregation in Harlem, the Abyssinia Baptist Church. Powell's early life was a storybook existence to black folks. The family's life was comfortable, secure, warm, loving, and affluent; they even had a summer home. Powell, Jr., attended Colgate College where he lived the life of the blue stockinged. This privileged existence did not create a snob, however. Instead, he dedicated himself to rescuing his people from racism and oppression and helping them realize their potential to have a better life.

Powell was sworn into the House of Representatives in the 79th Congress on January 4, 1945. It was the height of the Second World War, and black servicemen were fighting and dying for Americans at home in the segregated armed services. At the same time, all over the world the United States was preaching the virtues of the Four Freedoms advocated by President Franklin Roosevelt. However, the Four Fears Americans harbored against African Americans overrode their humanity and gratitude to black servicemen who risked their lives on the battlefields of the world for them.

Powell observed the hypocrisy and irony as he was being sworn in. In the nation's capital, and in fact, right there in the halls of Congress, African Americans could not eat, sleep or enjoy many of the privileges the United States was defending for foreigners due to racism and seg-regation. Furthermore, the District of Columbia, the city then 50 per-cent black, had no voting privilege and today, 80 percent black, the cit-izens still have limited voting privileges.

Powell won election to Congress on promises to: push for fair racial practices; eliminate restrictive covenants and discrimination in housing; pass the Fair Employment Practices Commission (FEPC); abolish the poll tax; make lynching a federal crime; end segregated transportation; protest defamation of any groups; fight against impe-rialism and colonialism; and strengthen the thirteenth through the fif-teenth amendments to the Constitution. He joined the other lone black Congressman, William L. Dawson from Chicago.

Speaker of the House Sam Rayburn talked to Powell shortly after he arrived and asked him not to "throw any bombs," to just take it easy at first. Powell replied that he had a bomb in each hand and intended to throw it. Rayburn almost died laughing.[21] Powell exhibited the type of courage and guts that people have to respect even if they are fearful.

Pampered and spoiled, Powell faced the real world of racism in col-lege when his best pal and roommate left him a note saying he couldn't live with him any longer. He had just discovered that Powell was "a Negro," when his minister father defended Negroes during a speech in the Chapel at Colgate University. Colgate' University officials agreed with the roommate's decision and moved Powell out of the room.

Although Powell had white skin and Caucasian features, he was one of the staunchest defenders of his race in the Unites States history. Ultimately, he paid a steep price for his commitment. Yet, when you see pictures of his mother, father and sister, the absurdity of race based on "blood" highlights the depths of the white superiority psychosis. It is quite obvious the Powells were the slave master's descendants who chose not to "pass" for white.

Another example of racist madness is exposed in his autobiogra-phy. Powell relates how "Robert Todd Lincoln, son of the emancipator," (sic Powell, 32) who hated and despised black people, acted out his mania. Todd frequented a restaurant where Powell worked, and whenever a recognizable black person touched the door of Todd's chauffeured car, he would reach out and rap the person on the knuckles with his cane. The manager asked Powell if he would open the door for Lincoln instead. "I, whose father had been raised by a branded slave, would open his door. And Mr. Lincoln, looking at my white hand, was satisfied."[22] For this "white" service, Todd paid Powell a dollar a day and the Inn's management gave him an additional ten dollars a week.

After leading the typical white, playboy college existence, Powell bombed out of the university before graduating. After several more attempts to become an attorney, one day he said he had a spiritual revelation when he heard a voice that led him to the ministry, and he eventually graduated from Colgate. He joined his father, Adam Clayton Powell, Senior, in the pulpit of the Abyssinia Baptist Church, the largest black church in New York. Abyssinia, renamed Ethiopia, is the earliest Christian nation in the world. "Long before the first Anglo-Saxon had passed a comb through his matted hair, long before the first Anglo-Saxon could read or write, the people of Abyssinia had accepted the institution of Christianity and had developed a culture," said Powell.[23]

In an incident similar to the one that led to the establishment of the first black church in the U.S., Mother Bethel A.M.E. founded by Richard Allen in Philadelphia, Pennsylvania, in 1794, Abyssinia Baptist was founded when a group of African traders sought to worship in the house of the Lord. They were ushered into the slave gallery; those sophisticated, well educated, proud world travelers left in protest. A white minister, the Reverend Thomas Paul, joined them. According to Powell, they pooled their resources, bought property and established the Abyssinia Baptist Church, the first non segregated Baptist church.

One hundred and fifty years later Powell's father, a remarkable man, had a vision for African American liberation in 1911, said Powell. He was in the vanguard of establishing Harlem as the black Mecca. At that time most black New Yorkers were situated in downtown areas around the forties, the site of the first Abyssinia church. Powell, Senior, insightfully saw them being squeezed out by business development, just as it is done in black communities today. He influenced the church membership to purchase land on 138th Street between Seventh and Lenox Avenues. He pitched a tent and preached to packed houses until he raised $340,000 to build the church!

In a well established, historical pattern, whereby whites maneuver to gain control of black institutions by giving money and demanding control over policies, John D. Rockefeller, Jr., the foremost "Robber Baron" of the time, offered to pay off the church's $60,000 mortgage if he could name the board of trustees. This pattern prevails today in well known black organizations, but, Powell, a man of great integrity and faith along with his board of trustees, had the morals and courage to turn down the leading financial mogul of the time. "Within four and a half years the church was free and clear of any mortgage and also from any outside control," said Powell.[24]

Another towering son of Africa also had the foresight of Powell, Sr., who pitched his church tent next door to Marcus Garvey's black Freedom Hall. Powell, Junior, said that one of the greatest thrills of his life was to sit at Garvey's feet or roll down Seventh Avenue with him as he paraded in his white plumed hat. Garvey, said Powell, shook up the U.S. when he set up the black United States within the United States. He landed in Harlem in 1914 saying let us have our own black empire because the U.S. will not let black folks have judges, mayors, etc.; in essence, they were prevented from self determination. Garvey had his own black cabinet, army, nurses, newspaper, steamship line and religion with a BLACK GOD! Garvey was the President. "Marcus Garvey was the first man to ever make 'black' Negroes proud of their color," said Powell.[25]

Abyssinia Baptist church became a model, a beacon for black churches. With the advantages and opportunities open to African Americans today, how many can equal Powell's record established at the height of Jim Crow, lynchings, and the Depression? For example, before Social Security, the church bought a home for members unable to work to live out their old age free of charge! Annually they contributed to the Foreign Mission Board, black colleges, and even gave financial help to any new church in Harlem. They established a school of religious education under the supervision of Columbia University. Adult education provided elementary English, citizenship, designing, dressmaking, home nursing, business courses and a school of dramatic arts. The community center, built as part of the main building, "was packed basement to rooftop morning and night throughout the week," said Powell.[26] Eventually the ten room penthouse apartment his father had built atop the church for his family was turned over to the church activities due to crowding. The original membership of seven hundred ballooned to twelve thousand during Powell, Jr.'s tenure.

Powell's audacity, political genius and unswerving dedication to the people of Harlem and people of color in the world made him a political threat to the power structure because of the Four Fears. But one act by Powell, more so than many others, went into the files that are kept by the unseen forces that patiently and systematically undermine African and African American leaders. They gather evidence, use sinister operations and other tactics which eventually destroy them. That act was his attendance at the Bandung Conference held in Indonesia in 1955.

A meeting of twenty-nine independent Asian and African nations led to the formation of the largest bloc in the United Nations. Powell foresaw the significance of participating in a conference that affected two billion people of color. He spoke to Congress expressing his sentiments, saying a team of U.S. citizens, both colored and white from various religious denominations should attend as observers. The purpose would be to let the conference know that "America is a democracy of the people."[27]

Powell wired the President suggesting a good-will mission be sent. He was shocked when he was merely afforded a copy of a White House memorandum saying the United States would not participate and "Congressman Powell should not be encouraged...to attend as an observer." When Powell announced that he would attend at his own expense, "all hell broke loose."[28]

Despite efforts from numerous influential sources to prevent him from going, he succeeded in attending the conference. In response, the

Administration ordered Powell, a United States Congressman, to stay away from the United States Embassy, the United States Ambassador and all United States employees in Indonesia! Powell's action brought to light that the United States had no foreign policy regarding Asia and Africa because they derived their policy from colonial powers.

Powell resorted to addressing Congress prior to his departure, explaining his wish to attend the conference for peace and to strengthen the brotherhood of the world. At the close of the speech, members of Congress rose to praise him, and "only then did the Department of State offer to give some assistance."[29] As it turns out they did so because of fear of the Communists exposing the Embassy for ignoring Powell "because he represented a minority."[30]

He took off for the conference assured that he would receive cooperation from the embassies. "In fact this was another Department of State lie," said Powell: "Not a single person from my government was there to meet me, not a citizen, but a Congressman, a senior Congressman of twelve year's standing, a ranking member of the Committee on Education and Labor and a member of the Committee on Interior Affairs. Never to my knowledge has the United States government let down a member of the United States Congress more completely than it let me down and, in so doing, let down all the American people...."[31]

Despite the snub, the humiliation he faced, and the international criticism of the United States for refusing to even send a message of good will to the conference, Powell defended the United States at a press conference when Communists attacked the United States for its racial policies. Powell said he had learned there was tremendous discrimination and segregation practiced by colored peoples in southeast Asia and anti-Semitism Oriental style. (Earlier Powell was criticized by Pan Africanists when he let the government send him on a good will mission to Africa "to combat Communist propaganda" at the same time Paul Robeson was being denied a passport. The true purpose of Powell's mission to Africa was to defuse accurate news reports by the Soviet Union on racism in the U.S. Aware of the intent of Powell's mission, Robeson, wisely moved to file a petition with the United Nations written with his friend William L. Patterson on behalf of all African Americans charging the United States with "genocide." Contrary actions by Powell labeled him in some quarters as a chameleon and questioned his sincerity.)

Powell also mistakenly took upon himself to influence the Bangdung Conference to take pro Western positions on certain resolutions. He returned to a "hero's welcome," to top level, off-the-record meetings with key people in the State Department even though Powell charged the U.S. "missed the boat" at the conference. Furthermore, although Eisenhower had ignored Powell's pleas and overtures before the conference, after his pro U.S. impact on the conference, he was granted an audience with Eisenhower. For all Powell's efforts and Eisenhower's promises to take meaningful action toward the peoples of Africa and Asia, nothing was done.

Nevertheless, Powell said the Bangdung Conference was a turning point for him. Until that time he aimed at doing all he could for Negro rights in the U.S.; after the conference, he began to see the necessity for a "new Afro-Asia bloc which was blocked by the crass stupidity and ignorance of our State Department."[32] Before, he had seen civil rights as the main method to save African Americans, now he saw civil rights as the "sole method by which we could save the entire United States of America." They were the yardstick by which "not only black Africa and brown Asia, but also white Europe were measuring our land."[33]

Exposing U.S. and colonial policies and influence, as in the case of Paul Robeson and W.E.B. DuBois, Powell set himself up for elimination. It would take time and it would take patience, but it would be accomplished. Not even Powell would suspect that it would be accomplished by one of his own.

As is often the case in history, it took a simple event to start actions that roller balled into a major problem for Powell. And, as is often the case regarding African American people who attempt to educate and liberate their own, the connection between the police, the FBI and world wide interests was unearthed. The whitewashing of the murder of a black serviceman by two New York policemen put Powell to work seeking justice. He was stonewalled, and after getting nowhere with the local Grand Jury, he asked the FBI to investigate. It was not until "Frederick Woltman, ace reporter for the *New York World-Telegram & Sun,* published the shocking truth."[34] There was an agreement between the Department of Justice and the New York City Police Department under J. Edgar Hoover to keep the FBI from investigating New York City's sordid record of police brutality."[35] After the *New York Times* picked it up and published an editorial calling for an investigation of police brutality, Powell became the target of a vendetta that ultimately cost him his position in Congress and possibly his life.

Powell had to take the case to the Congress before it received the appropriate action. "Meanwhile, I received anonymous telephone calls and letters saying that one day the Police Department, the career and Civil Service men in the Department of Justice would get me for what I had done," said Powell.[36] The police commissioner was fired but the Congressional report on the case was tabled and no one could get hold of the report, according to Powell. Sinister acts against Powell escalated after that.

The numbers racket was a haven for crooked cops, politicians, lawyers, etc. Powell complained that more Negro than white number men were being arrested in Harlem. The larger problem was that Negro bankers who once controlled the numbers were either being muscled out by white racketeers or being made to work for them.

Powell touched off a fight against "the Mafia, the syndicate, and the Combine," when he reported on the connection between the police and the racketeers in Congress.[37] "When I did this, the police closed down, within thirty-six hours, numbers drops and arrested one hundred and five people..." only in Powell's district.[38] This opened cans of worms that disclosed relationships between selected attorneys and gamblers, "the legitimizing of the millions of dollars from policy rackets right out into the normal channels of trade and finance."[39] Just as it happens with the drug trade today.

The sinister sources started to close in on Powell when again a small event led to a calamity. Powell was deftly using the United States

Congress to expose the unholy alliances between gangsters, the police, lawyers, and business by reading his charges into the Congressional Record. He named a black woman, Esther James, who was allegedly extorting money from gamblers and numbers operators and turning the money over to the Police Department. She took the place of a policeman Powell had initially revealed as the "bag man for the police." He also put into the Congressional record the name of a police sergeant who quickly resigned; soon after, many others hastily quit.

Powell received threats on his life, but he charged ultimately, that it was not done with guns or bombs, it was done through the courts. Esther James sued him for defamation of character for one million dollars. James won her case which sent him on round after round of appeals. Charges against Powell snowballed after that. The government charged him with income tax evasion. His church records were subpoenaed eight years after the period in question and his wife's tax records were brought into play. A special task force was set up in the Justice Department. Powell's back and forth alliance with Democrats and Republicans, and his legendary skirmishes and eventual support of Eisenhower were all issues to take into consideration when sizing up the forces that led to Powell's downfall. He was placed on a pit and turned slowly as the coals were heaped on the fire.

However, when Congress stripped him of his seat, Powell had the great joy and gratification of having his Harlem constituents refuse to elect another person to his seat. For two years they chose to go unrepresented. Before it ended, the sinister forces succeeded in running him out of Congress, and his audacious support of the black Power movement further increased the fear and alienation against him.

Powell charged that crooked voting allowing him to be replaced by another black man, Congressman Charles Rangel. Powell's love for his supporters, prevented him from subjecting them to a long court battle during which time they would go without representation. In addition, he suffered from serious physical, life threatening ailments that sapped his strength, and his personal troubles mounted but he never lost his resolve to fight for his people. Many parallels can be drawn between him and Paul Robeson, W.E.B. DuBois, Muhammad Ali, Malcolm X, Martin Luther King, Jr., Denmark Vesey, David Walker, Charles Diggs, Mike Espy, Al Hastie, Marcus Garvey, well known and not so well known African American men. The legacy of vendettas perpetrated against African and African American men lies in the hearts of those who cower in fear of the Four Fears. Powell was a mighty foe who had to be eliminated but whose life and spirit reign throughout time and the ages. Those entities dedicated to enslave and eliminate people of color to maintain white superiority are but ignominious dross and only have the satisfaction of their deeds for minutes in time, while great black men's deeds live on eternally as shining examples for posterity.

Malcolm X

The murder of Malcolm X was planned to appear as though "A Black Man Did It." However, it was not the normal pattern of accusing a faceless black man of a crime to cover up for a white criminal. Malcolm's murder was under the influence and direction of religious charlatans, sinister national and international powers. Black men did actually carry out the assassination before the eyes of horrified loyal followers that fateful Sunday in the Audubon Ballroom in New York City. The murder was orchestrated to appear as though members of the Nation of Islam were the sole perpetrators; however, it has been rumored and documented that the FBI and shadowy foreign powers were behind the killing and took advantage of the rift between Malcolm and Elijah Muhammad. *Judas Factor*, one of the most definitive investigations of the murder of Malcolm X to date, reports from fifteen years of research and hundreds of interviews. Based on an examination of 300,000 pages of FBI and CIA declassified documents, the book analyzes "the role the intelligence community played in instigating the death of the Nation of Islam's most revered and feared leader."[40] The forces behind Malcolm's murder took advantage of the practice of making black men scapegoats. Thus, the murder of Malcolm became the ultimate example of a scapegoat for he was killed by scapegoats to scapegoat black men in general.

Malcolm X possessed extraordinary qualities as one of the greatest men in history: fearlessness, brilliance, intelligence, leadership, confidence, vision, humanness, political consciousness, energy, foresight, audacity, spirituality, assertiveness, wit, youthfulness and charm. He was also a gifted orator who identified with the dispossessed and used religion to motivate the hopeless.

Malcolm represented the triumph of manhood. He said what black men wanted to say to white men. Either because of conditioning, intimidation, political reasons or religious prohibitions black men had been kept from speaking out for their manhood. "Vicariously through him some Negro men got up off their knees for the first time in their lives and touched their manhood as if it were a new Christmas toy."[41]

Before his conversion on a trip to Mecca that caused him to reject the separation of the races, he publicly advocated that black people disconnect from their American oppressors. Whites have consistently separated from blacks, constructing white nooses around black communities, suburban around urban, as well as in politics, jobs, education, religions, economics and society as a whole. Yet when Malcolm dared to tell African Americans they would be better off if they separated and worked toward self determination, he became a threat to the nation.

Malcolm personified manhood and became an example for other black men. His manly attributes extended far beyond America's shores. He dared to go abroad to reevaluate his position. When he observed men with white skin acting as decent humans, not judging him by his color or his race, Malcolm moved towards an international example of manhood and a symbol for the oppressed people of color worldwide. An African American man with his extraordinary talents was a threat to international powers controlling colonized peoples; therefore, he had to be eliminated when he moved to expose American and European complicity in enslaving people of color.

As he traveled Malcolm became more knowledgeable, less subjective with a new universal awareness Ossie Davis notes, "No one who knew him before and after his trip to Mecca could doubt that he had completely abandoned his shock effect statements, his bristling agitation for freedom in this country not only for blacks, but for everybody."[42] However, Malcolm's metamorphosis did not diminish him one iota, instead it was the mark of a truly great man. He did not completely abandon his beliefs, he just admitted his vision was limited to his constricted view from the restrictions of his experiences in America. "...I never doubted that Malcolm X, even when he was wrong, he was always the rarest thing in the world among us Negroes: a true man."[43]

Malcolm's placing the plight of the American black people before the U.N. put him in the same jeopardy as two of his stalwart predecessors who were dedicated to racial equality, Paul Robeson and W.E.B. DuBois. Like Robeson, he was mysteriously poisoned while abroad but managed to survive. Robeson had his passport lifted and his earnings slashed because he filed a 240 page petition with the United Nations charging the United States with "genocide." DuBois was arrested and charged with Communist activities at age eighty despite his age and contributions to the United States throughout his life.

In 1964, if Malcolm had persuaded the Afro-Asian bloc to include the civil rights struggle and to charge the United States with colonialism in U.N. debates, the African nations might have gained leverage for the emerging African nations. This black man with an eighth grade education was about to create havoc in the United States–Africa policies. "Activities by the FBI and the CIA suggest that the intelligence community was determined to abort this eventuality by any means necessary."[44]

Martin Luther King, Jr., and Malcolm were moving toward détente. J. Edgar Hoover had wire tap evidence that King and Malcolm were on the verge of forming an alliance, heard June 27, 1964. This action played a role in stiffening the resolve of Hoover, who had a personal vendetta against black people in general, to destroy black civil rights movements. When Malcolm formed his Organization of Afro American Unity (OAAU), after leaving the Nation of Islam (NOI), he announced that "...every effort would be made to form a coalition with Dr. King, Roy Wilkins (NAACP), James Farmer (CORE), and other civil rights groups."[45] Putting it all together—Africa, Middle

East, and the United States civil rights organizations—made Malcolm a more formidable foe of international white supremacy than Marcus Garvey and his organized five million black members in the UNIA which was crushed by the U.S. government.

Malcolm's father had been an active lieutenant in the UNIA, and a fervent supporter of Garvey. Although Malcolm, his siblings and his mother suffered after the mysterious brutal death of his father under the wheels of a street car, Malcolm in his first six years of life, had the advantage of conditioning from his Garveyite parents. At their side he learned about the injustices and subservient conditions of African Americans, the terror of the Ku Klux Klan (suspects in his father's death) and the brilliant plans of Garvey to liberate African Americans. Malcolm's innate intelligence and correct early education, at home and in school, combined to create a man inspired by God and supported by the universe.

Despite the harsh conditions he endured as he was tossed from foster home to institutions when his mother had a breakdown, and despite falling into petty crime during his early life, his well known conversion to an exemplary life while in prison is further testimony to his unique character. Imprisonment proved to be the discipline needed to harvest his innate abilities; free of the traditional education system, it was a blessing as well. Dr. Amos N. Wilson, developmental psychologist, said a history and experience make a people and Africans cannot use someone else's history and experience to teach others.[46] Traditionally, education in the U.S. has been a tool used to maintain white dominance. "black people are taught to be dumb by the education system. The idea of an oppressor giving education for freedom is ludicrous," said Wilson.[47] Thus, Malcolm's early education and his later street smarts, untainted by American formal education, made Malcolm's self taught prison education more effective.

Since the educational system is an integral part of the American system, Malcolm's opinion of the American system and black people's indoctrination is appropriately applied to the educational system. Like Wilson, he said the American system, including education, was developed for the enslavement of black men. Only drastic changes will change it.

> ...a chicken cannot lay a duck egg because the chicken's "system" is not designed or equipped to produce a duck egg...The American "system", political, economic, and social (and educational) was produced from the enslavement of the black man, and this present "system" is capable only of perpetuating that enslavement....In order for a chicken to produce a duck egg its system would have to undergo a drastic and painful revolutionary change...or Revolution.[48]

After his assassination, Malcolm the imposing, larger-than-life man, was vindicated by his earlier adversaries and extolled by heads of state, the masses around the world, in numerous book, articles, and mass media. It was inconceivable during his life, but his autobiography is required reading across racial lines throughout the United States. However, out of the element in the white university system that harbors racial superiority cane a detractor, Bruce Perry, a University of Pennsylvania professor who spent twenty years writing a book to tarnish Malcolm's image and legacy even in death. The extent and depth of his venture, often present in white men's fears of African American men, apparently sustained him for twenty years as he labored to discredit the world renowned hero.

Perry conducted nearly 400 interviews, searched out Malcolm's grade school records,[49] his family's history,[50] prison records, FBI and other secret government files.[51] The complimentary sounding book title is a ploy to draw in reader then expose them to Perry's contrivances and speculations. His observations were biased; he used news articles and government reports that substantiated his slants regarding Malcolm. He also tended to discredit other black men unless they were Malcolm's enemies. For example. he devoted lots of attention to Malcolm and Adam Clayton Powell's relationship, and throwing barbs at Powell. Furthermore, Perry reported unfair accounts of Malcolm's life that portrayed Malcolm as a fraud from a dysfunctional family. "Thus, although Malcolm maintained that he 'never' bit his tongue... he had been keeping mum about the improprieties of his skirt-chasing father, his lonely-love starved mother and his criminally inclined half-sister," said Perry.[52]

He cites many blacks who gave him information about Malcolm. However, Betty Shabazz, Malcolm's wife, revealed her wisdom that implied suspicion of Perry's motives before Malcolm's death when she refused to talk to Perry about him. He tried to interview her about her attendance at the Mosque after Malcolm was silenced by Elijah Muhammad. Perry states, "Mrs. Shabazz declined to let me ask whether Malcolm wanted her to attend in order to demonstrate his loyalty to the Nation of Islam. Nor did she grant me an opportunity to ask her anything else." [53]

Despite his efforts, Perry's book was not a top seller. It was released around the time of Spike Lee's film "X". An exceptional media blitz including front page headlines announcing the film almost rivaled the reception of Alex Haley's "Roots." Malcolm's eminence, black power and the media campaign overshadowed Perry's attempts to tear down Malcolm. His public statements, in retrospect, given the tenor of the government at that time, foreshadow that his demise by violent means was inevitable. In 1963 he said: "We have a common enemy. We have this in common: We have a common oppressor, a common exploiter, and a common discriminator. But once we all realize that we have a common enemy, then we unite—on the basis of what we have in common. And what we have foremost in common is that enemy—the white man. He's an enemy to all of us. I know some of you all think that some of them aren't enemies. Time will tell." [54] Much has been made over Malcolm's reformation after his exposure to other races abroad, and he reevaluated his feelings about whites. However he did not change his opinion about the forces in power. Near the end, mysterious events led him to believe sinister forces outside of the Nation of Islam were involved in plots to kill him. Ironically, it was black men who actually murdered him. Malcolm was the most feared African American man of his time. In death, he has gained more respect and prominence than before. Fears led to his murder, but fears could not stain memories of him and what he accomplished in his short life.

Contemporary Black Scholars

The challenge that African American male scholars present to the American Academy is most revealing. What is this fear of African American men in the university arena? Why has the response to them often taken harsh uncompromising positions, even when the university preaches diversity of opinion? During the 90s, the fear of the black male scholar turned in intellectual issues such as the role of ancient Africa in the development of Greece, the place of homosexuality in the ancient European and African worlds, Affirmative Action, the new radical right, and the post modern ideas of multiple consciousness.

Nearly one hundred years ago, William E.B. DuBois, one of the best known African American scholars, as mentioned before, had been denied a regular appointment at the University of Pennsylvania. Then, this was part of a larger problem the society had in dealing equitably with black intellectuals. DuBois with all of his brain power was inevitably nothing more that another black man in the eyes of the whites of that time who viewed him through a racial prism. All things were reduced to race, and those who prevented him from teaching at the University of Pennsylvania at that time have many cohorts in other universities in contemporary American at this time.

In a number of American universities, African American men have been hounded by relentless attacks on their scholarship, personalities and even their social commitment. One sees the attacks on black men in the academy increasingly in the form of administrative fiat against those in positions of influence and authority within the university. It appears that any African American male dedicated to expressing the agency of black people's interests, in nearly every situation, is targeted for intellectual assassination. Furthermore, the inability of the white academic community in America to allow the emergence of an authorative Afrocentric position in the academy is indicative of what has historically happened in American society.

African American scholars who question the hypocrisy of the society are often victims of the worst types of abuses and attempts at discreditation. Those who engage in the abuses and discreditation are railing to make the heroic black scholars appear as though they are insane, irrational, unreasonable and incompetent. Yet, African American intellectuals are the most dynamic vanguard the Black community has in the field of knowledge. It is knowledge that is vital to their survival. African American scholars, male and female, untethered to the guardians of white supremacy, are the correct interpreters of the events, personalities, and phenomena that makes Africans and African Americans who they are.

In the past decade prominent African American scholars such as John Blassingame, Tony Martin, Molefi Asante, Leonard Jeffries and David Bradley have come under severe attacks by university committees, deans or provosts, and some vicious news reporters. The academic culprits also use delaying tactics such as holding up prompt responses to vital issues in question regarding the black scholar if the matter is counter to their biases. Through great tribulation, including being drawn away from their scholarship and other duties to address the attacks on them, most of the named black scholars have managed to survive within the university. (David Bradley of Temple University, whose independence threatened many in white academe, is an exception.) Furthermore, the fact that those under siege have differing political philosophies, has not spared them from the lash of the whip or other cruel punishment if they do not conform to the various codes of conduct created for the university's purposes. At the heart of the matter is fear of the black intellectual's power.

The forces of white supremacy have seldom wanted to see the rise of an independent black male intelligentsia and extraordinary efforts have been put in place to defame them, particularly those in the Afrocentric Movement. Herein is the battlefront of the future as we enter the 21st century. African Americans must be vigilant that the aims and interests of the black community are not sabotaged by synchophants and provocateurs from within the race and those outside forces committed to destroying independent thinking black intellectuals. Behind the challenges to black intellectuals is a contest for the right to define the agenda of the black world. The right is engaged in a desperate attempt to maintain a strangle-hold on people of color to continue to exploit them and their resources, here and in Africa, but primarily to maintain white supremacy.

To document their presence, to give recognition to their achievements and to hail their courage, the following listing is most of today's major African American male scholars: Na'im Akbar, Elijah Anderson, Molefi K. Asante, Daudi Azibi, Amiri Baraka, Jake Patton Beason, Yosef ben-Jochannan, John Blassingame, David Bradley, Anthony Browder, James Brunson, Jan Carew, Jacob Carruthers, John Henrik Clarke, Legrand Clegg, II, Caine Hope Felder, Charles Finch, John Hope Franklin, Nathan Hare, Asa Hilliard, Leonard Jeffries, Kobi Kambon, Maulana Karenga, Richard King, Baba Zak A. Kondo, Jawanza Kunjufu, C. Eric Lincoln, Acklyn Lynch, William Mackey, Haki Madhubuti, Manning Marable, Tony Martin, Thaddeus Mathis, Anthony Monteiro, Edwin J. Nichols, Wade Nobles, Runoko Rashidi, James Smalls, William Strickland, Oba T'Shaka, James Turner, Ivan Van Sertima, Linn Washington, John A. Williams, Robert Williams and Conrad Worrell.

8
Sexuality
▨▧▨▧▨▧▨▧▨

Penis and color envy of African Americans have long been themes in literature, myths and religion. The Europeans reduced people of color to beasts and relatives of apes as this justified their own bestial, vile trade in human flesh and stolen resources. The roots of these widely held beliefs, however, are still prevalent and have led to castrations, literally and figuratively. Fear of African American men's virility and the color of their skin have regularly been the main reasons for murdering and maiming them. Myths, lies, castration and comparison to beasts from the earliest recorded times until the present are behind the most frightening of the four fears of white men—sexual fear of black men.

It's widely believed that black men have larger genitals than whites. This belief, true or not, has been associated with fears of black genetic dominance and elicits images of African and African American men wiping out the white race. These fears have been behind most of the dastardly acts perpetrated against black men down through the ages.

As Africa's human and natural resources were disclosed, more and more vicious lies were invented to financially support European countries and to build the United States. Using the Ham myth and citing black as evil, white explorers reported that African rituals, culture, religion, language, government and life styles were "heathen, ungodly, and ruled over by savages." African men were frequently described as Dixon described them later in the *Clansman*, "brutish or beastly." Since they were animals, treating them like cattle was acceptable. "The Guinea Company instructed Bartholomew Howard in 1651, to buy and board as many niggers as [the] ship [could] carry along with the cattle."[1]

The murdering, raping slavers from Europe allegedly first saw anthropoid apes at the same time they saw Africans, and thereafter speculated they were related. However, the facts prove that they were relating to their own historians. Edward Topsell's *History of Four Footed Beasts*, 1607, described apes as "so venerous that they will ravish their women."[2] Baboons were also described as lustful, and a French king who had one said that it "...above all loved the company of women and young maidens, his genital (sic) member was greater than might match the quantity of his other parts."[3] Pictures of two varieties of apes graphically emphasized the "virile member." Europeans for centuries promulgated bestiality and conjectured widely about bestial copulation.[4] Therefore, they merely foisted onto African men their own lascivious practices and fantasies.

Topsell also made explicit and persistent connections between apes and the devil. Association of apes...with devils was common in England. James I linked them in his *Demonology,* (1597): "The inner logic of this association derived from uneasiness concerning the ape's indecent likeness and imitation of men it revolved around evil and sexual sin, and rather tenuously, it connected apes with Blackness."[5] Some went so far as to say Africans sprang from apes and apes were the offspring of Negroes and some unknown beast. These wild, racist tales were broadcast around the world by ignorant as well as learned white men. "By forging a sexual link between Negroes and apes...Englishmen were able to give vent to their feelings that Negroes were a lewd, lascivious and wanton people."[6] Even Leo Africanus, a Moor converted to Christianity, no doubt influenced by the Old Testament wrote that his black brothers were "brutish, destitute of religion and laws."[7] Whose laws? Europeans' laws? Africans certainly did not survive for thousands of years without laws.

The myths were invented after Europeans and Easterners made forays into Africa and discovered her vast riches. Therefore, murdering, enslaving, and plundering were justified because it was all right to take what belonged to "animals" since they weren't human. This was not the case, however, before U.S. slavery. In *The Voyage of M. Gerogre Fenner*, Walter Wren said "...although the people were Blacke (sic) and naked, yet they were civill" (sic).[8]

In *Sex and Race*, J.A. Rogers reveals little publicized facts about early contacts between African men and white women.[9] Rogers first points out that most primitive Africans thought the most so called beautiful white woman was ugly. This was before white media promoted white women throughout the world as the epitome of female beauty. Today, unfortunately in many places in Africa it's reported that women are using harmful products to lighten their skin. They do so, they say, to please African men who are mesmerized by white women because of western propaganda invading Africa through movies, television, advertising, and the glorification of white women in sexy picture magazines.

Written in 1940, using very well documented sources, Rogers states in *Sex and Race* that contrary to reports and innuendoes that Africans lusted after white women, in fact, Africans and Asiatics shunned sexual contact with white people. Africans were extremely courteous and "the farther away from so called civilization, the more courteous the population [the Africans were]."[10]

The truth of the matter is exposed by Rogers' revelation of sexual imperialism that accompanied international economic and political imperialism by white men. History does not report comparative ravaging and raping by Africans. A white women traveling in West Africa alone reported that no African male ever dreamed of molesting her even when she was alone. Again it's a case of white men deceitfully accusing black men of acts practiced by their own kind.

Affairs between native women and white men were due to the white men's power and superior military strength. Rogers quoted from Pierre Mille, a leading French writer on colonial subjects, regarding the reality of white men and native women interaction. Mille reviews Le Decivilise by De Renel: "…It happens often enough that the European who has experienced a union, marriage or concubinage with a native woman is no longer able to experience…conjugal peace with a woman of his own race.…If by caprice…or out of simple exotic curiosity, he has relations with one of these women, he can no longer leave them alone. This is what he finds…that he can no longer live with a white woman."[11] Conversely, a French army surgeon who spent twenty-eight years among natives in Africa and the West Indies studying their sex lives said that "the African woman does not love the white man because the latter is incapable of satisfying her sexually."[12] This is a rather broad statement; nevertheless, even if universally untrue, the fact that it is a widely held belief, stokes the sexual fears of white men. It causes reverse accusations that black men are the brutes lusting after white women.

Furthermore, in truth it's reported that white women's hatred of black women was even stronger than white men's hatred of black men. "It is no race question that brings about this unchristian feeling in her. Here the struggle is a sexual one; for life and death."[13] The white woman who saw a black rival as "that dirty, stinking, infected creature is now on an equal plane with her."[14] On the other hand, there were white women who seduced their black house boys, sometimes with the husband's tacit approval, with him off somewhere with *his* black woman.

Africans and Asians were very strong in their prohibitions against race mixing, and went to great lengths to ostracize those who married and brought foreigners into their society. On the other hand, whites, liberal in race mixing abroad, were viciously hypocritical about miscegenation at home in the United States, and Europe. Rogers said, "Another significant fact about the first slaves spirited from Guinea is that they were not all full-blooded Negroes. Some were fair and mulattos as well as black."[15] This corroborates that white men had relations with women of color prior to the infamous European enslavement. Their behavior was contrary to the egalitarian race mixing which occurred throughout the world before the colonial explorations and invasions of Africa and nations of color. For example, the Moors who seized Spain in 711 A. D. were married to Portuguese women; this was validated by Rogers.[16]

Sex and Race documents reveal how England and the United States, while proclaiming democracy and equal justice for all, were busy creating monsters of African men and marketing that image to the rest of the world. All this took place during the period of slavery and is still in vogue. Before slavery, Africans were integral to the world and world knowledge.

For millennia, Africans traveled and migrated throughout the world. They were merchants, explorers, conquerors, soldiers and even novelty figures in European courts, especially for white women of royalty. The evidence is overwhelming that African men were sought after for their sexuality by white women throughout Europe. African men mesmerized men and women with their exotic features, strength and intelligence. Furthermore, they were widely accepted in every aspect of life until the Europeans and Americans started the nefarious slave trade. All of the complex lies to excuse and justify white's evil, avaricious activities were hidden under the propaganda mill operating against Africans and African Americans.

J. A. Rogers, who was ridiculed and scorned for his research of African history during his lifetime, wrote well documented and cogent histories of Africans and their intermingling with whites on equal terms. He states, "Racial doctrines as they exist today (1940) negate intelligence. Indeed they furnish a paradox that exceeds any of the extravagances of Gilbert and Sullivan."[17] The purpose of *Sex and Race*, Rogers says is to "see what have (sic) gone into the making of this fearsome creature"—the black man.[18]

Adolf Hitler's quest for world domination was rooted in white superiority. According to Rogers, "it is a matter of common knowledge that Hitler copied very carefully American racial tactics."[19] Arch Nazi, Rudolph Hess, said in the *New York Times*, before the Second World War and the attempt at Jewish extermination, that he defended his stand on racial discrimination by saying, "We are very much like the Ku Klux Klan."[20] The Ku Klux Klan was Hitler's role model. In

America, the Klan, a bunch of lowlife cowards hiding under white sheets, singled out black men as their primary foes to intimidate and eliminate because of the Four Fears.

People are governed by myth not reality emphasized Rogers. The Klan operated on the myth that black men were half human, savages, rapists and brutes out to lure and ravage white women. While in America and across the seas, consensual sex relations between white and black existed from recorded time and perhaps even before. As stated before, interrelations flowered until the discovery of the New World and Africa's riches. Racial inferiority was invented to justify robbing and raping people of color.

Roger's research reveals that thousands of years before the slave trade in 384 B. C. Aristotle wrote about a white Sicilian woman who committed adultery with a Negro and had a daughter by him. "Not that this was an uncommon occurrence,"said Aristotle.[21] It was a problem only because adultery was punished by death.

In 46 A. D. Plutarch, first of the great biographers, speaks of a Greek woman who had a black child although she and her husband were white.[22] Here again adultery was illegal; therefore, the wife was placed on trial. To grant her reprieve, at the trial it was "discovered" that she was descended from an Aethiop (Ethiopian) in the fourth generation. Thus, the reason for the black child.

Hippocrates 460-359 B. C. reported a similar situation, but even more farfetched.[23] A noblewoman who was white, as was her husband, explained that her "coloured child" was due to a picture of an Ethiopian in the bedroom she and her husband shared. In another case, a woman said she simply "saw" a black man before she gave birth. Numerous lies were told by white women to cover up their cohabiting with black men. In fact, giving birth to black children became so regular that in 60 A. D. Juvenal advised Roman husbands to keep abortive potions on hands for their wives if they did not "want blackamoor children."[24] More directly, he told husbands to actually give their wives the potions themselves to be certain of eliminating black babies.

Epigrammatist Martial (40-120 A.D.) satirically wrote of the married Roman who had seven children.[25] One, the son of the cook, had wooly hair, another had a flat nose and thick lips, the image of a black wrestler, and two daughters were black and belonged to the farmhand.

Shakespeare borrowed from the Roman women's proclivity for black men in *Titus Andronicus*. Andronicus had an illegitimate black mixed race child. J. A. Rogers says that Shakespeare plucked his character from the court of Louis XIV. Louis' wife, Marie Theresa, gave birth to a black child. The queen had an African dwarf named Nabo. Africans such as Nabo and others were very popular in the courts of Europe and numerous paintings and tapestries from that era depict them. However, in Nabo's case, he mysteriously disappeared after the birth of the black baby. In addition, it was reported that the baby was a still birth. However, the enraged king spared the baby girl's life and she was named Marie Theresa and sent off to be raised away from court. She became a nun and was called the black Nun. Black nuns were honored and believed able to perform miracles because of their dark color.[26]

Perhaps the earliest recorded maligning of black men's sexuality was by Herodotus (484-425 B.C.), who said black men and East Indians (note they were also black) had black semen like their faces.[27] Aristotle disagreed with Herodotus saying black men's semen was white. (The question by this author is how did they find out the color of black men's semen?) For centuries later partisans of the two argued pro and con about whether it was possible for a white woman to have a black child without cohabiting with a black man. These disputes were utter denials of the relationships between white women and black men by the converse parties.

An important conclusion disclosed by Rogers is the fact that these early contacts between white women and black men elicited no hostility toward black men which is so characteristic of English, American, and German writers of 1940, especially when the white woman was involved. Class and religion were the important concerns, not race. White supremacy is, and has been, all encompassing, inundating

143

every aspect of life in the United States. It is extremely difficult, therefore, to envision a society where a person's class and religion were factors that led to trials and punishment. Whites' responses to skin color, sexuality, intelligence, strength and anger of African American men and youth are the causes of manifold methods of impugning, debasing and criminalyzing them.

CASTRATION

Scientific racism, anthropologic lies that Africans were biologically related to apes, and that like apes, black men lusted after white women, were lynch pins on the African captives when they were drug ashore in the United States. To validate the lies, racist interpretations of the Noah myth in the Old Testament were preached (see Genesis 9:18-26). These contentions concealed the lust, greed and guilt of the slavers and helped to lay the grounds for events that eventually led to the atrocious practice of castrating slaves, lynchings and instances of false jailings.

The historic scenario invented by white men and women set the stage for justification of demonizing black men. Initially, for a short time, it shocked and outraged the world when castration was a lawful punishment in the Carolinas, Virginia, Pennsylvania, New Jersey, Bermuda and Antigua. It was reserved for African Americans and rarely for Native Americans. White men were included for a while in the 1700s, but later the laws were worded to apply to Negroes—free or slave in some colonies. "Castration was a legal punishment crafted by Americans....The specifically sexual aspect of castration was so obvious as to underline how much of the white man's insecurity vis-a-vis the Negro was fundamentally sexual."[28]

Frantz Fanon in *Black Skin, White Masks* compares how differently Jews are thought of in terms of castration:

> No anti Semite, for example would ever conceive of the idea
> of castrating the Jew. The Jew is killed or sterilized, but the
> Negro is castrated. The Negro is killed because the symbol of

manhood is annihilated which is to say that it is denied. The difference between the two attitudes is apparent. The Jew is attacked in his religious identity, in his history, in his race, in his relations with his ancestors and with his posterity; when one sterilizes a Jew, one cuts off the source; every time that Jew is persecuted, the whole race is persecuted in his person, but it is, in his corporeality that the Negro is attacked. It is as a concrete personality that is lynched. It is as an actual being that he is a threat. The Jewish menace is replaced by the fear of the sexual potency of the Negro.[29]

In the prior Colonial period, the same accusations about African men's sexuality had been promoted amongst whites. Just as before, the accusations were used to conceal the white men's proclivity for African women. "...It is apparent that the white men projected their own desires onto Negroes, their own passion for Negro women was not acceptable...and not readily admissible," said Fanon.[30]

Other scare tactics inflamed the issue. *The Psychology of Colonization*, Dominique O. Mannoni, Prospero and Calihan reported that racialists widely use the argument: If you had a daughter would you marry her to a Negro? "I have seen people who appear to have no racialist fears lose all critical sense when confronted with this kind of question."[31] Mannoni contends the reason is because of the father's incestuous feelings and they turn to racialism as a defense reaction. Fanon says, "Granted the unconscious tendencies toward incest exist. But why do they emerge with respect to the Negro? Why not, for instance, conclude that the father revolts because in his opinion the Negro will introduce his daughter into a sexual universe for which he does not have the key, the weapons or the attributes."[32]

Furthermore, charges Fanon, "the civilized white man retains irrational longing for unusual eras of sexual license, of orgiastic scenes, of unpunished rapes, of unrepressed incest....Projecting his own desires onto the Negro, the civilized white man behaves 'as if' the Negro really had them....Throughout the history of white men conquerors over black men have functioned this way."[33] Europeans as well as American white men have this fear of black men, not only due to their sexual potency, but because of the white man's incest and longings for exotic experiences according to these experts.

White men suffer from "Negrophobia" reports Fanon. "The Negro symbolizes the biological danger. The Negroes are animals, apes, cannibals. And 'whoever says rape says Negro.'" His research findings after questioning 500—whites, French, German, English, Italian—were gathered as he operated in his capacity as a psychiatrist. Fanon gained their confidence, and when they were secure and relaxed, he would insert the word Negro in an associative test.[34] Sixty percent of their replies related to the Negro biologically: penis, strong, athletic, potent, boxer, Joe Louis, Jesse Owens, Senegalese troops, savage, animal, devil, sin. Furthermore, when Fanon had his European colleagues administer the test, the numbers jumped *upwards* of 60 percent.

During crises, times of slave revolts or rumors of revolts, reports that black men would kill all white people except the young white women whom they would save to rape mushroomed. It's noteworthy that there were never any documented reports of black men seizing and raping white females. These scurrilous lies were largely unique to the United States and increased the dangers of living under slavery in the United States. In the West Indies, for example, the attitude towards race mixing was not as rigidly racist as in the United States, therefore, there were fewer laws and sanctions against African men.

However, the Europeans exported to the United States the preoccupation with the African American men's genitals. On these shores the concept of the African American male as sexually aggressive was reinforced by what Europeans called "their anatomical peculiarity" being in possession of an especially large penis. The rumors fortuitously coincided with the firmly established idea of the Negro's sexuality and was "salt in the wounds of white men's envy." The irony of this matter is that in reality the white man was using the African for stud service to produce children for unpaid labor. Obviously, the white men's fears were generated by their own guilt and anxiety about their economic security as well as their sexually weak genitals and aggressive minds. On the other hand, tales circulated about Native Americans' anatomy made special notes that their penises were smaller than the Europeans. It is also interesting that Europeans never circulated vicious stories about Native Americans being rapist to the extent they did regarding African Americans.

In *Black Skin, White Masks*, Fanon recites a parody on black men's penises that aptly portrays the absurdity of the white man's fears. He says first that the European culture has an image of the Negro which is responsible for all the conflicts that arise. On the influential movie screen the image is "faithfully reproduced." Furthermore, "even serious writers have made themselves its spokesmen," says Fanon, quoting Michel Cournot, Martinique (1948).

> The black man's sword is a sword. When he has thrust it into your wife, she has really felt something. It is a revelation. In the chasm that it has left, your little toy is lost. Pump away until the room is awash with your sweat, you might as well just be singing. This is good-by....Four Negroes with their penises exposed would fill a cathedral. They would be unable to leave the building until their erections had subsided; and in such close quarters that would not be a simple matter....[35]

Fanon concludes that when one reads this passage over and over and lets oneself go, "...one is no longer aware of the Negro but only of a penis. The Negro is eclipsed. He is turned into a penis. He is a penis."[36] Cournot's parody was to replenish the inflammatory fables and specious images of black men's phalluses.

On the other hand, Dr. Frances Welsing in *The Isis Papers—The Keys to the Colors* offers a definitive theory of sex and color as the two primary factors threatening whites. Dr. Welsing's point of view: "white envy of the black phallus is addressed unconsciously when whites constantly concern themselves with the comparative size of the black phallus versus the white phallus....Any school child could suggest that a simple tape measure can settle the question once and for all, unless the questioners and 'researchers' are afraid to measure."[37]

"If it is not the length of the penis, then it is the sexual potency that impresses and strikes fear in white men," says Fanon.[38] Quoting Etiemble, he concludes: "Racial jealousy produces the crimes of racism. To many white men the black man is simply that marvelous sword which once it has transfixed their wives, it leaves them forever transfixed."[39] Thus, the argument is here that African American men's sexuality is one of the four major causes of the intractable forces to control and eliminate black men. These factors are the reason for the continuous attacks, imprisoning and attempting to destroy African American males. Whites use every means to maintain white supremacy due to their nightmarish fears of domination and annihilation by people of color.

Dr. Welsing says, "The extreme rage vented against even the idea of a sexual alliance between the black male and the white female, which has long been a dominant theme of white supremacy culture, is a result of white males' intense fear of black males' capacity to fulfill the greatest longing of the white female—that of conceiving and birthing a product of color."[40] Black males who have engaged in sex with white females report on the frequency of white females expressing a desire to have a black baby. Furthermore, Welsing, a psychiatrist, says that her knowledge reveals the reason black males' testicles are attacked the most in lynching (and beatings by white men and white police) is because the testicles store the color producing genetic material.

Welsing reports on her theory of white preoccupation with black men's penises: "The repeated and consistent focus on the size of black males' penis by both white males and females is due to a 'displacement factor'. Since the fact of color envy must remain repressed, color desire can never be mentioned or the entire white, psychological structure collapses. Therefore, attention is displaced to a less threatening object or symbol—the penis."[41] She says her analysis of the genetic threat the black male penis portends can be appreciated when reviewing lynching records. "...The major percentage of black males who were lynched by white males had their genitals attacked, removed and taken away by white males (i.e. carried them on their person)."[42] This behavior is peculiar to white males in relationship to men of color. Welsing interprets this behavior as fear of the black male genitalia. Thus it must be attacked and destroyed. Furthermore, "there is envy and a desire for possession of same."[43] An extreme, but relevant example is the case of Jeffrey Dahmer, the white male who lured seventeen black men to his home, murdered them, had sex with them when they were dead, cooked and ate them. "These dynamics are at the root of the fear of all competition white males feel towards black males, thus preventing true competition in all areas of people activity: economics, education, entertainment, labor, law, politics, religion, sex and war," concludes Welsing.[44]

Andrew Hacker, a white professor at Queens College, New York City concurs in his book, *Two Nations, Black And White, Separate, Hostile, Unequal.* He says that sex and race fears are the main defense for segregation and the entire caste order. Hacker quotes from Gunnar Mydral, who observed over fifty years ago in *An American Dilemma*, that white men insisted they had to protect their women from advances of black men. "Hence, periodic lynching, often preceded by castration."[45]

Hacker comes closer to the real reason for the castrations as explained before. He says, "Compounding the ordinary insecurities most men have in this sphere, white men face the mythic fear that black men may out rival them in virility and competence...aggravating this unease is a further foreboding: that white women may wonder whether black men could provide greater sexual satisfaction than they now get from their white mates."[46] On the other hand, says Hacker, white women may be asking themselves what draws white men to black prostitutes?

Welsing's color and penis theories tie in more complex psychological issues than Hacker, but they are not far apart in their understanding of the hypocrisy in white supremacists' responses to African American men.

An explanation of Welsing's color confrontation theory postulates that white people are a small minority of the world's population, about 25 percent according to the *Washington Post.*[47] Further, white is actually the absence of color. "I," she says, "reason then, that the quality of Whiteness is indeed a genetic inadequacy or a relative genetic deficiency state, based upon the genetic inability to produce the skin pigment of melanin" (which is responsible for all skin color).[48] She concludes that color is normal for human beings and the absence of color is abnormal. Color always "annihilates" non color and therefore Europeans respond psychologically fearfully when confronted with people of color. Conscious or unconscious, it is, she says, manifested throughout history. And because black people have the most color, they are the most envied and feared.

Whites' deep desire to have color is evident in the way they flock to beaches and tanning salons. No matter that sun exposure due to ozone depletion is causing record numbers of skin cancers and tanning solutions are proving harmful, whites persist in trying to get colored. Some blacks also try to change their skin color to white. The fundamental difference is that they are the victims of conditioning to white supremacy, evidence of identification with the oppressor.

9
Anger

Because of the level of violence committed by some young black males at this time, there is a tendency to view their expressions of anger through a narrow or bigoted prism: *they are prone to be that way because they are black males.* Along with mimicking their oppressor's behavior, as mentioned in this book, oppressed people are more violent with each other than their enemy. In addition, the massive government campaign to destroy the protest movement of the '60s and '70s caused young black men to forsake protesting. They were led into the even more dangerous mine fields of illegal drugs as the mass media played the Pied Piper by creating cravings for short term riches, power and instant gratification.

Despite the media's negative portrayals of young black males, it must be recognized that they are neither the majority, nor the average. Furthermore, across the United States manifold programs initiated by black men are operating to save black youth. Anger from frustration, hopelessness, and injustice in every aspect of U.S. life has been working against black men and youths since 1600, yet legions of brave, committed African American men and women have fought and died to provide freedom and justice to the very ones who are killing each other. Their forefathers may have been less educated, but at least they knew who was the real enemy.

Be assured, the carnage strewn across the cities of the U.S. by blacks against blacks will run its course. History is a testament that movements run their course. Those in power in academe, politics, business, etc., realize this phenomenon; it is reason to redirect the economics of the inner cities from the drug culture to the prison economy culture. Eventually those killing each other will see they are fodder for the prison economy. The question is: where will the anger turn then?

The focus on angry black men at this juncture is to discuss some of the important angry African American men who expressed and demonstrated their ire at the system, not by killing each other for monetary gain, or misperceived slights, but by disciplined, brave acts. Those black pioneers expressed their anger with brilliance in written documents and protests in the face of seemingly insurmountable odds.

Prohibited in many places from learning how to read and write under the threat of death, flogging or other vicious punishment, African captives were constrained from putting their protests in writing. Therefore, it is a remarkable testament to their heroism, intelligence, and strength that the early protests against the evil system of slavery were not only written, but circulated.

David Walker, a free man because his mother was free, was born in North Carolina in 1785. At age 30, he settled in Boston and became a clothing dealer. Walker also became a leader in the Colored Association of Boston and was the agent for the abolitionist newspaper, *Freedom's Journal*. In 1828, he wrote the first of four articles known collectively as

"Walker's Appeal." "The 'Appeal' is by far the most articulate militant work of its time. It implores, threatens, curses. One moment it is afire with burning vengeance, demanding the white man's blood, and the next it softens with the hope the white man will change."[1] Walker's articles created a frenzy. In the south where a ship was quarantined that carried the pamphlets to Savannah, Georgia, a secret session of the legislature made it a capital offense to circulate literature that might incite slaves to revolt. A bill was passed with a reward of $10,000 for Walker captured alive, and $1,000 if dead! Louisiana reacted with a bill expulsing all free slaves who settled there after 1825. Nat Turner's slave revolt in 1832, was linked to Walker's "Appeal". Quaker abolitionists condemned it, taking their traditional non violent line. The "Appeal" was truly directed to his black brothers and sisters, squarely placing responsibility on them for their freedom.

"Would they fool with any other people as they do with us, No, they know too well that they would get themselves ruined." Walker said the Asians would tear them from head to foot. Indians would not rest day or night; they would be up all times of night cutting their cruel throats. "But my color, (some, not all) are willing to stand and be murdered by the cruel whites..."[2]

Slave revolts were inevitable. Living with repressed animosity is bound to erupt in revolt. Eventually the deepest fears of the individual owners and the guardians of the institution of slavery came to life despite the extreme sanctions, threats of death and harm to slaves and their family members. For instance, "... a plot in Louisiana amongst the slaves in 1732, possibly with Indian allies. In retaliation, a female slave was hanged and four men were broken on the wheel. Their heads were then stuck on poles at the upper and lower ends of New Orleans as grim and stark inducements to docility."[3] Even in the face of such consequences, black men and women, with great valour, still organized revolts; others revolted by escaping in thousands of numbers. Among the better known leaders are Denmark Vesey, Gabriel Prosser, Nat Turner and Harriet Tubman. The take over of the slave ship *The Amsted* by Africans and the renowned Underground Railroad movement illustrated the power of the organization of slaves. Living among black traitors who spied on them and told the authorities took even greater courage and resourcefulness.

As late as the 1960s and 70s some white historians continued to downplay the repressed anger, slave revolts and their extent. These historians aimed to continue the lie that Africans were content and docile and those who revolted were basically mad men. The Pulitzer Prize was awarded to William Styron for *The Confessions of Nat Turner*, 1968. Styron's fictionalized account was focused on emasculating and making Turner into a deranged black man fantasizing about white women, but so aberrated, that Turner was only capable of a homosexual relationship. Loyle Hairston, one of the ten prominent African American writers who responded to Styron's diatribe, states, "As though bedeviled by white-supremacist-inspired fears of the black man's alleged superhuman sexual powers, William Styron triumphantly reduces his slave to a religious celibate—a kind of self castration. Poor Nat Turner's only sexual experience is—alas!—a homosexual one!... This is pure racism. Slaveholders themselves could not have dredged up more repugnant notions about the 'nature' of black men."[4]

Herbert Aptheker, in a 1963 reissue of *American Negro Slave Revolts* writes, "Generally speaking, this book weathered some heavy attacks launched by individuals to whom white supremacy and the magnolia-moonlight-molasses mythology that adorns it were sacred. Still, neither this or the notoriously radical political sympathies of its author have succeeded in consigning the work to damnation–that is to oblivion."[5]

John Henrick Clarke, ed. of *Ten Black Writers Respond* said that the respondents collectively agreed that the distortion of Turner's character was due to the racial climate of the period of the 1960s in which urban revolts were prevalent.

Anger over being discriminated against by the white religious establishment was the catalyst for the origination of early black churches and most other organizations that refused African American men membership. For example: The Elks, Masons, Odd Fellows, etc. Richard Allen, Absalom Jones and William White were praying in a white church in Philadelphia when church officials dragged them from their knees and ejected them. The ignominy and outrage of the rousting from the church aroused indignation and anger in the men and they started the African Methodist Episcopal Church. Still standing on the original site, Mother Bethel A.M.E. is a national historic site. The constructive use of anger by black men growing from inequity and unfairness led to the formation of the strongest and most formidable black institution. Fear of influence of the black church has been behind the bombing and firing of black churches throughout the years.

Attacks and prohibitions against black people in the white press caused the initiation of the formerly powerful black press. Founded in 1827, *Freedoms Journal*, the first African American newspaper, was to allow African Americans to plead their own cause. Black people had to pay to get their stories in the white press and suffer the abuse of attacks in white newspapers such as *The Enquirer*, edited by Mordecai M. Noah. Garland Penn, a black journalism historian, writes "the attacking paper was edited by an Afro-American hating Jew who encouraged slavery and deplored the thought of freedom for the slave and made the vilest attacks upon the Afro Americans."[6] *The Rams Horn*, started in 1847 by Willas A. Hodges, came in reaction to the *New York Sun's* editorializing against black suffrage. When Hodges attempted to have his reply published he had to run a paid advertisement. His ad was modified and Hodges protested the changes, he was told "the Sun shines for white men and not for colored men."[7]

Frederick Douglass' newspaper, *The North Star*, joined the angry band. Douglass attacked slavery in every form, including print. He also had to fight his white abolitionist allies who said the Constitution was pro slavery. Douglass used his oratorical skills along with his writing to publicize his cause. His famous, angry anti-Fourth of July speech is a legendary indictment of the lack of full freedom for African Americans that remains true today. In Douglass' early life, slavery was the major method of controlling African American men. Ever since, unjustly applied laws have kept them disproportionately in bondage. Incarceration is the most brutal and inhumane way that whites assuage their guilt in general and, specifically, their fear of the potential retaliation from black men.

George Jackson responded to his unwarranted excessive prison sentence: "Hurl me into the next existence, the descent into hell won't turn me. I'll crawl back to dog his trail forever. They won't defeat my revenge, never, never. I'm part of a righteous people who anger slowly, but rage undamned. We'll gather at his door in such number that the rambling of our feet will make the earth tremble."[8]

At the tender age of eighteen, Jackson was sentenced to one year to life for stealing seventy dollars from a gas station! For nearly seven years of the next eleven years he was held in solitary confinement. "Surrounded by armed oppression, without freedom of movement or terrain, George Jackson assumed the task of revolution in prison, wherever he was and by any means necessary—prisoners' unions, strikes, self-defense, teaching, writing in constant struggle against oppression."[9] Jackson's ability to withstand the savage deprivation in solitary confinement caused him to say that calamity had hardened him and turned him into steel. Jackson and African American men like him who face, tolerate and endure the most depraved, psychologically sordid, debased sentences, yet return to say that they were strengthened by their ordeal produces terror in their captors. At twenty-eight, Jackson was charged with murder of a guard in the infamous Soledad Prison. Similar to the case of former journalist Mumia Abu-Jamal under death sentence for allegedly killing a white policeman, Jackson gained international attention and acclaim. He was said to be the most powerful and eloquent voice since Malcolm X and dangerous because he was a symbol of courage for the oppressed people of the world. Jackson and his brother became identified with the revolutionary struggles of that time. Soledad Brothers incarcerated with Jackson included Ruchell Magee, Fleeta Drumgo and John Cluthchette.

Jackson was shot in the back while allegedly attempting to escape, killed by a San Quentin prison guard, August 21, 1971, two days before his trial. Prison officials reported that "Jackson hid a 32 ounce, 8 inch long pistol and 2 clips of ammunition in his medium sized Afro hair style before he was searched 'nude' and then walked 100 yards with a guard before the pistol was detected...."[10]

His poignant letter from prison is a prophetic, intrepid lament:

> If I leave here alive, I'll leave nothing behind. They'll never count me among the broken men, but I can't say that I'm normal either. I've been hungry too long, I've gotten angry too long often. I've been lied to and insulted too many times. They've pushed me over the line from which there can be no retreat. I know that they will not be satisfied until they've pushed me out of existence altogether. I've been the victim of so many racist attacks that I could never relax again.... I can still smile now after ten years of blocking knife thrusts, and the pick handles of faceless sadistic pigs, of anticipating and reacting for ten years, seven of them in solitary. I can still smile sometimes, but by the time this thing is over, I may not be a nice person. And I just lit my seventy-seventh cigarette of this twenty-one hour day. I'm going to lay down for two or three hours, perhaps I'll sleep....From Dachau, with love, George.[11]

Like George Jackson, Mumia-Jamal had an early encounter with the police that would have lasting consequences. Mumia writes that as a youth of fourteen he went to the the police for help and got beaten instead of helped. As a result, "I was beaten into the Black Panther Party." Later as a journalist, Mumia wrote stories critical of the police handling of a 1978 raid on a house where members of the back to nature organization, MOVE, was opposed by neighbors because of their lifestyle in an urban neighborhood. Mumia was not involved at the time of the raid but subsequently became a MOVE supporter. The infamous, racist of record, former police chief and Mayor of Philadelphia, Frank Rizzo, is alleged to have had a vendetta against Mumia because of his reporting on the raid. At the time of the police raid MOVE members were huddled in the basement below ground. The police were above ground and the alleged trajectory of the bullet that killed the police officer was downward. The day after the raid, Rizzo ordered the house bulldozed to the ground, destroying all evidence. Nine MOVE members are still serving life sentences for the death of the policeman. In 1985, after a protracted confrontation with police at another location, and complaints from neighbors, government forces bombed the house and had orders to let it burn. It burned to death eleven MOVE members, including five children. Only one child and one adult escaped. Not one police person, city, state or other official was sentenced to prison.

The night of the shooting of the police officer Mumia was driving a taxi in downtown Philadelphia and came upon his brother being beaten by the officer. In the ensuing altercation Mumia was shot in the stomach and beaten on the head by police. New evidence unearthed by a new attorney alleges the bullet that killed the officer was different from the gun Mumia had a permit to carry. Mumia has been on death row for thirteen years in a rural Pennsylvania prison. For five years he has been writing commentaries published in forty newspapers in the U.S. and Europe, as well as featured in a *Yale Law Journal* article. In June of 1995, the new Republican governor, Tom Ridge, kept a promise and signed his death warrant for August 17, 1995. It sparked protest in several cities in the U.S. and abroad where many organizations have been supporting freedom for Mumia. Petitioning for a new trial and appeals are in process.

Parallels to other racial militants who expose injustices and confront the system are labeled angry and dangerous. George Jackson and Mumia Abu-Jamal join the ranks of their great African American hero ancestors wading in or watching and directing the struggles from another plane.

> Perhaps I'm naive, maybe I'm just stupid—but I thought the law would be followed in my case, and the conviction reversed. Really...I continue to fight against this unjust sentence and conviction. Perhaps we can shrug off and shred some of the dangerous myths laid on our minds like a sec-

ond skin—such as the "right" to a fair and impartial jury of our peers; the "right" to represent oneself; the "right" to a fair trial, even.

They're not rights—they're privileges of the powerful and rich. For the powerless and the poor, they are chimera that vanish once one reaches out to claim them as something real or substantial. Don't expect the media networks to tell you, for they can't, because of the incestuousness between the media and the government and big business, which they both serve. Even if I must do so from the "valley of the shadow of death," I will.[12]

From death row, this is Mumia Abu-Jamal, December 1994.

James Baldwin was the premier and dominant voice of anger who used his brilliant writing as an essayist, playwright and novelist to expose with moral outrage the social and political conditions infecting African Americans. Baldwin says:

Negroes want to be treated like men: a perfectly straightforward statement, containing only seven words. People who have mastered, Kant, Hegel, Shakespeare, Marx, Freud, and the *Bible* find this statement utterly impenetrable. The idea seems to threaten profound, barely conscious assumptions. A kind of panic paralyzes their features, as though they found themselves trapped on the edge of a steep place. I once tried to describe to a very well known American intellectual the conditions among Negroes in the South. My recital disturbed him and made him indignant; and he asked me in perfect innocence, "Why don't all the Negroes in the South move North?"

They do not escape Jim Crow: they merely encounter another, not-less-deadly variety. They do not move to Chicago, they move to the South Side; they do not move to New York, they move to Harlem. The pressure within the ghetto causes the ghetto walls to expand, and this expansion is always violent. White people hold the line as along as they can, and in as many ways as they can, from verbal intimidation to physical violence. But inevitably the border which has divided the ghetto from the rest of the world falls into the hands of the ghetto. The white people fall back bitterly before the black hoard; the landlords make a tidy profit by raising the rent, chopping up the rooms, and all but dispensing with the upkeep; and what has once been a neighborhood turns into a "turf." This is precisely what happened when the Puerto Ricans arrived in their thousands—and the bitterness thus caused is, as I write, being fought out all up and down those streets.[13]

We Charge Genocide

The Crime of Government Against the Negro People was filed by Civil Rights Congress, 1951 with the United Nations, in Paris, France. At the same time, a delegation led by Paul Robeson filed copies with the Secretary General of the U.N. in New York. It is a document framed out of the anger at the unremittent racism to instigate action against the inhuman treatment of African Americans. William Patterson, a leader in the petition movement, said in 1970 that it was unwise to expect the U.N. to force the U.S. to adhere to the U.N.'s stated goals and principals. However, it was worthy to charge the U.S. with racism before the world to mobilize action. Evidence of genocide was documented in the Petition with six years of incidences covering twenty-one pages pulled from the black press, the NAACP, Urban League, concerned social and legal agencies. The voluminous record included every section of the U.S.: including beatings, shootings, murders, intimidations, mental cruelty, terrorism, mob violence, wrongful imprisonment, and threats of all sorts. Complicity in genocide was charged against the President, Congress, the Supreme Court of the

U.S., the Attorney General of the U.S., the Department of Justice, State and local officials, corporate interests, such as the Rockefellers, Morgans, DuPonts and Mellons, the Ku Klux Klan, governors, senators and representatives.

The reprint of the Petition in 1970 found more to report adding to the 1951 charges. The preface by Ossie Davis states:

> We Charge Genocide! indeed we do, for we would save our-selves and our children....We do not need to wait until the Dachaus and Belsens and Bunchenwalds are built (Nazi death-prison camps) to know that we are dying. We live with death...not so obvious as Hitler's ovens—not yet. But who can tell?
>
> ...As long as we stayed in (our) place there at the bot-tom—we were welcomed...But a revolution of the pro-foundest import is taking place in America. Hard, unskilled work—the kind nobody else wanted, that made us wel-come...in America...is fast disappearing.
>
> ...What will a racist society do to a subject population for which it no longer has any use? Will America in a sudden gush of reason, good conscience, and common sense reorder her priorities?—revamp her institutions, clean them of racism so that blacks and Puerto Ricans and Native Indians and Mexican Americans can be...meaningfully included on an equal basis?...Or, will America grow meaner and more desperate as she confronts the just demands of her clam-orous outcasts, choose genocide?[14]

Davis concludes by asking the question we in 1990s are facing. He asks will America build a world of racial and social justice or try the fascist alternative—a deliberate policy on a mass scale, of practices she already knows too well, of murderous skills she sharpens each day in Vietnam, of genocide, and final, mutual death? Vulnerable and youth-ful, they valiantly challenged the age old institutionalized injustices in the South. Their resoluteness in the face of vicious attacks on them undoubtedly was a motivating force in the minds of the renewed petition to the United Nations charging the government-supported genocide against black citizens.

The African American protest movement owes much to the black college students. Those who struggled were the backbone of the Civil Rights Movement of the 60s. Their angry but nonviolent protests and lunch counter sit-ins against discrimination were in the vanguard of the massive resistance and Martin Luther King's rise to martyrdom and greatness.

Greensboro, North Carolina sit-ins by high school and college students in February of 1960 spread to fifteen cities in five Southern states. Eventually black students engaged in numerous demonstrations for justice in all aspects of the movement. Black students, who were angry over black studies being omitted from the curriculum in schools, included their institutions in the protest struggles along with lunch counter sit-ins.

When the Southern Christian Leadership Conference gave the Student Nonviolent Coordinating Committee (SNCC) $800 to organize sit-ins, it was indirectly the birth of the Black Power Movement. In the fall of 1961, SNCC had a staff of sixteen, by 1964 they had a working staff of 150. Black and white students took the famous Freedom Rides and were attacked, imprisoned and beaten for their heroic efforts. In 1963 they formed the Mississippi Freedom Democratic Party with a slate of candidates, black and white, to gain seats in the national Democratic Party Convention. These young people with directed anger were mobilized and effective as well in their voter registration drive.[15]

An irascible, 23-year-old philosophy student, a graduate of Howard University, Stokely Carmichael, was elected chairman of SNCC. Soon thereafter, James Meredith, a young black man, enrolled in the University of Mississippi. Whites rioted and federal troops were called out. Meredith was shot when he marched to prove he could do so, unmolested. After the shooting, matters took a change. Carmichael said that only "black power," not marching would stop the southern bigots and murderers from their vengeance.

The Black Power cry was grabbed by the militant wing of the movement as their clarion call. However, it was met with resistance and fear among blacks and whites. Martin Luther King ran a full page ad in the New York Times condemning Black Power. The idea of blacks with power was totally incongruent to whites—also many blacks.[16] The press went crazy with speculation and sensationalizing the issue. J. Edgar Hoover went out of his mind and the invention of the KGB, Nazi-like Counter Intelligence Program (COINTELPRO) was fired up. When SNCC and the Black Panthers, barely out of their teens seeking food and justice for their people, joined forces the edict went out to smash them by all means. SNCC and the Panthers were portrayed as angry young thugs, categorized by Hoover as the most dangerous threat to the U.S.—superceding the U.S.' arch enemy, the Russian communists. Thus all of the Four Fears of white men came out when African American, intelligent, strong, and angry, youth organized to liberate their people.

The Howard University student protests disclosed the hidden white hands behind black institutions of higher learning. Dr. Nathan Hare, who was expulsed from Howard for his role in the uprising, went to San Francisco State College. A five month struggle for black studies ensued and Dr. Hare was also fired from San Francisco State.

After waging many battles, black studies were started in varying degrees in colleges and universities. However, a concomitant effort has not been successful in grade schools. The related Afrocentric movement is struggling on choppy seas of resistance from the same American Federation of Teachers Union that has opposed inclusion of black studies since 1960. Dr. Nathan Hare's prognostication about new black faculty was basically correct.

"There were many conclusions—both at San Francisco State and at Howard—which have implications for students everywhere...For one thing, the ancient Toms at Howard are being replaced now...by a liberal black bourgeoisie....The group of which we speak is a radicalized sector of the new black middle class, leaning neither toward the left-wing Panthers nor the radical separatists such as the Republic of New Africa....They stress cultural activism, while almost totally disdaining the politics of confrontation; few have ever participated in any form of activist struggle. Thus, despite their puffy tooting of "blackness" and the concomitant cover of black unity, they continue to receive strong criticism from their more revolutionary students."[17]

It appears that the majority of the black faculty hired as a result of the black students activism have acted as Dr. Hare perceived. Aside from scholarly papers for a select audience of experts, articles in journals, and scads of conferences going at the colleges' expense hardly a squeak is heard regarding black students' problems with the administration or faculty. Nor rallying to confront the politicians stripping education and financial aid programs not to mention the almost complete avoidance of interacting with and supporting the black communities in which many of the urban colleges and universities are located. "...The San Francisco State struggle, the longest and most intense in college history, though not the most publicized, did help radicalize colleges and students throughout the nation."[18]

Fear of Anger in African American men was centered on Malcolm X before his assassination, very similar to the attention given to Louis Farrakhan. Living through both eras one hears statements echoed. Malcolm X was depicted as angry and dangerous. Many African Americans who lived during his time were as scared of him as the whites.

Speaking to a group of teens from Mississippi, sponsored by SNCC, at the Hotel Theresa, New York, December 31, 1964, Malcolm spoke to them on being nonviolent:

> This is one of the things that our people are beginning to learn today—-that it is very important to think out a situation for yourself. If you don't do it, you'll always be maneuvered into a situation where you are never fighting your actual enemies, where you will find yourself fighting your own self.

164

I think our people in this country are the best examples of that. Many of us want to be nonviolent and we talk very loudly, you know about being nonviolent. Here in Harlem, where there are probably more black people concentrated than any place in the world, some talk that nonviolent talk too. But we find that they aren't nonviolent with each other....They are nonviolent with the enemy. A person can come to take your home, and if he's white and wants to heap some kind of brutality on you, you're nonviolent; or he can come take your father and put a rope around his neck, and you're nonviolent. But if another Negro just stomps his foot, you'll rumble with him in a minute; which shows you that there is an inconsistency here.

I myself would go for nonviolence if it was consistent, if everybody was going to be nonviolent all the time....But I don't go along with any kind of nonviolence, unless everybody else not being nonviolent....But as long as you've got somebody else not being nonviolent, I don't want anybody coming to me talking any nonviolent talk. I don't think it is fair to tell our people to be nonviolent unless someone is out there making the Klan and the Citizens Council and these other groups also be nonviolent.[19]

Conclusion

The Four Fears of white men are hidden dynamics behind incalculable actions that negatively affect African American males. The fears are prodigious, historical and unabated. Today they are more difficult to verify because of the layers of hypocrisy that circumvent laws and other venues that expose resultant unfairness. In the last twenty-five years the crisis of African American males raised the question, "Are African American males an endangered species?" Numerous indices indicate the endangered status is a fact, and that means the entire African American populous is also endangered. The Four Fears are a significant component in this picture. African American men and women must escalate efforts to illuminate the problems and take organized action for change.

In the past thirty years great strides toward change were made on many fronts to alert African Americans to their objective and subjective conditions caused by discrimination and racial oppression. The movement to make African Americans knowledgeable about their history has been very effective. There is a revolution in book authorships and sales by and about African Americans and African history. Furthermore, African Americans are the primary consumers. Throughout the nation vigorous activities are aimed at correcting the misinformation and indoctrination in white history. A masterful undertaking, the Afrocentric movement to infuse and inform about African American culture and history is forging ahead in the face of opposition from many white educators. Another momentous turn of events is more African American male youths graduating from high school than ever before. And, inspite of the dire disclosures that more African American men are in jail than in college, it must be regularly publicized that more African American males are attending college than ever before. In addition, throughout the U. S. programs to rescue black male youths flourish. Now the Four Fears are brought to light in this book to help understand what has taken place down through the years.

African Americans: male and female, rich, middle class and poor, north and south, large and small organizations, churches, businesses, politicians, educators, institutions, etc. must also make survival first on every agenda and continue to keep the resolution of the problem of the Four Fears of White Men and related matters uppermost in their activities. Be as militant as the Jewish people are in reminding the world of their holocaust at every turn. African Americans must also uproot their own lassitude. Make all the circumstances that weaken and threaten African American society their objective to constantly devote efforts to vitiate impediments.

Although this book focuses on white male's fears of black men, it should not be construed as ignoring or downplaying the struggles of African American women. Haki Madhabuti constantly points out: men fear other men, they do not fear women. Therefore, men are the first line of attack. The unfortunate condition of many African American women in large part is due to the Four Fears of White Men because of the effects they have on black men. Since women are the closest to men, they are the most likely to be subjected to the fall out from the injustices, frustrations, anger and fears the men face. Furthermore, African American women suffer untold misery from the loss of suitable male partners due to the social engineering of black men. Perpetually it causes classes of men to be undereducated, unjustly imprisoned, unemployed, and unhealthy. These constituents are the major drain on African American families' stability and a peaceful, productive society. Restoration of African American men to their rightful places in their families and society, protection and guidance of African American boys, access to cultural awareness, history, formal education and religious cooperation will help to restore order, provide economic, political and social gains. In summary, it will alleviate most of the major problems confronting all African Americans. There are other crucial considerations involved too.

The Four Fears of white men and related racial animus extends beyond the boundaries of the U.S. The survival of America is tied into the survival of the African American male. In today's global village, economics, politics and human rights are enmeshed. Will the non white peoples of the world accept the extirpation of African Americans and still feel secure in their relationships with America? At this time China hurls back on America complaints about China's human rights' policies. In retaliation, China exposes the way America treats African Americans when America tries to convince the world that it is the leading example of democracy. Treading in the steps of Paul Robeson and Malcolm X, a delegation of African Americans is poised to present the predicament of African Americans to the world via the United Nations. This move is further evidence of generation after generation of African Americans' resiliency and ability to rise to meet adversity and propose viable solutions.

The adaptability of African Americans far exceeds their sojourn in America. Granted, this is a bleak period with numerous reports about the straights of African American males. Nevertheless, it must be kept in mind that fear harms the perpetrators more than the victims. It is up to the victims to realize this fact and to refrain from succumbing to their fears of the perpetrator's power. African Americans can exploit a remarkable, sound foundation that extends beyond present day Western domination. *In Fear of African American Men: The Four Fears of White Men* is another boulder in the foundation.

Notes

Chapter 1

1.   Gossett, 5.
2.   Williams, 315-16.
3.   Chalmers, 24.
4.   Dixon, *The Clansman, 290.*
5.   Gossett, 280.
6.   Ibid.
7.   Leab, 223-4.
8.   Wilson, 106-107.

Chapter 3

1.   Herrnstein and Murray, xxii, 2. Ibid.; 3, xxiii.
4.   Gossett, 156.
5-6.   Sharon Begley, "There is Not Enough," *Newsweek,* Feb. 13, 1995, 67-72.
7.   Ibid.; 8. Ibid.; 9. Ibid.
10.   Anthony Monteiro, *Philadelphia, New Observer,* April 5, 1995.
11.   Ibid.; 12. Ibid.
13.   Diop, 23; Ibid., 14, 15, 16, 24.
17.   Ibid.; 18-19. Ibid., 24-25.
20.   Adrian Collins-Translator. *The Inequality of Human Races.* New York: H. Fertig, 1967.
21.   L.A. Newby, 195.
22.   Putnam, Carelton. <u>Race and Reason</u>. Public Affairs Press, Washington, D.C., 1961.

Notes

23.   L.A. Newby, 195.

24.   Garrett, Henry E., "The Equalitarian Dogma," 257.

25.   Fischel, Jack, "Strange 'Bell' Fellows," Commonweal, February 10, 1995, 16-17.

26-7. Ibid., 17.

Chapter 4

1.   Peter J. Buxton on *Tony Brown's Journal*, 23, October 1994. Ibid., 2-12.

13.   *The City Sun*, New York, NY, December 15-21, 1993.

14.   *The Albuquerque Street, News*, Albuquerque, NM, July 16, 1993.

15.   *The City-Sun*, Ibid., 16-33.

34.   Ji-Ahnte Sibert, Anthony and Denise. "Medical Repression." Z *Magazine*, May 1994, 17-20.

35.   Ibid., 17-53.

Chapter 5

1.   Higginbotham, 66.

2.   McIntyre, 163. Ibid., 3-5.

6.   Linn Washington. *The Philadelphia New Observer*, June 14, 1995.

7.   FBI, 1992 Crime Report.

8.   Statistical Abstracts, 1994.

9.   Ibid.

Chapter 6

1.   Ashe, 3.

2.   Ibid., 6.

3.   Ibid., 9.

4.   Ibid., 53.

5.   Newby, 12, 13.

6.   Ibid., 19.

7.   Ibid., 20.

8. Ashe, Ibid., 16.
9. Ibid., 20.
10. Ibid., 19.
11. Ibid., 20.
12. 13. 14. Ibid., 27.
15. Ibid., 30.
16. 17. 18. Ibid., 31.
19. Ibid., 32.
20. Ibid., 33.
21. Ibid., 34.
22. Ibid., quoted in Finish Farr, op cit., p.82 by Ashe.
23. 24. Ibid., 35.
25. Ibid., 36.
26. 27. Ibid., 37.
28. 29. 30. Ibid., 38.
31. 32. 33. Ibid., 39.
34. 35. Ibid., 41.
36. Rust, 246.
37. Ali, 114; 38. Ibid., 115; 39. Ibid., 166; 40. Ibid., 146, 147; 41. Ibid., 367.
42. Michael Lind. "Our Jury System Isn't Sacrosanct; There are Better Ways to Injustice," *New Republic*, October, 1995, 10.
43 44. 45. Ibid., 13.
46. Faulkner, 28.
47. Ibid., 49.
48. Ibid., 55; 49. Ibid., 54; 50. 51. Ibid., 62.
52. Ibid., Book Jacket.
53. Ibid., 166; 54. Ibid.; 55. Ibid., 199.

Chapter 7

1. Clarke, 3.
2. Ibid., 4.
3. Ibid., Robert A. Hill in Clarke, 49, 53: Garvey in Clarke 86: Clarke 96, 9.

4. Ibid., 164.

5. Ibid., 150.

6. Logan, Rayford W., ed., What the Negro Wants, W.E.B. DuBois, "My Evolving Program for Negro Freedom," 38.

7. Hamilton, 118,119.

8. Ibid., 118; 9. Ibid., 75.

10. Robeson, 8; 11. Ibid., 8; 12. Ibid.; 13. Robeson, Appendix 113.

14. Ibid., 19; 15. Ibid., 20; 16. Ibid., 31; 17. Ibid., 63.

18. Patterson, vii.

19. Robeson, 109.

20. Powell, Book Cover.

21. Ibid., 72; 22. Ibid., 33; 23. Ibid., 46; 24. Ibid., 52; 25. Ibid.,51; 26. Ibid., 22; 27-28. Ibid., 103. 29-30. Ibid., 105; 31. Ibid., 106; 32-33. Ibid., 118; 34. Ibid., 139; 35. Ibid., 140; 36. Ibid., 143.

37. Ibid., 146; 38. Ibid.

39. Ibid., 147.

40. Evanzz, Book Cover.

41. Clarke, Malcolm: The Man and His Times, 67.

42. Ibid., 130.

43. Ibid., 131; 44. Evanzz, 272, 273.

45. Ibid., 243.

46. Ibid., 177.

47. Ibid., 178.

48. Clarke, 304, 305.

49. Perry, xii.

50. Ibid., xiii.

51. Ibid., xiv.

52. Ibid., 232.

53. Ibid., 244.

54. Bietman, 5.

Chapter 8

1. Jordan, 28; 2. Ibid., 29; 3. Ibid., 4. Ibid., 30; 5. Ibid.; 6. Ibid., 32; 7. Ibid., 33; 8. Ibid., 5.

9.	Rogers, 146; 10. Ibid., 147; 11. Ibid., 143; 12. Ibid., 143, 144; 13-14. Ibid.; 15. Ibid. 156.

16.	Ibid., 151; 17. Ibid., Forward; 18. Ibid.; 19. Ibid., 1, 2; 20. Ibid., 2; 21-23. Ibid., 3; 24-27, Ibid., 4.

28.	Ibid., Jordan, 156.

29.	Fannon, 162-164.

30.	Ibid., 165; 31. Ibid, 169; 32. Ibid., 170; 33. Ibid., 165; 34. Ibid., 166; 35. Ibid., 169; 36. Ibid., 170.

36.	Welsing, 96, 97.

38.	Fanon, 171; 39. Ibid.

40.	Welsing, 6,7; 41. Ibid., 7; 42. Ibid., 97; 43. Ibid., 99.

45.	Hacker, 61; Ibid., 62.

47.	*Washington Post,* September 5, 1994.

48.	Welsing, 4.

Chapter 9

1.	Chambers, 54-55; 2. Ibid., 57.

3.	Aptheker, 182.

4.	Clarke, *Ten Black Writers Respond,* 71.

5.	Aptheker, Author's Preface to 1963 edition, 182.

6.	Woleseley, 18; 7. Ibid., 19.

8.	Jackson, *Black Scholar,* cover., 9. Ibid., 4; 10. Ibid., 2.

11.	Jackson, *Soledad Brother,* cover.

12.	Abu-Jamal, xviii.

13.	Baldwin, 67, 68, 69.

14.	Patterson, v, vi.

15.	Chambers, 212; 16. Ibid., 217.

17.	Hare, *The Black Scholar.* "The Battle for Black Studies," May, 1972, 32-47.

18.	Ibid. loc. cit.

19.	Malcolm X, 3, 4.

Bibliography

Akbar, Na'im. *Visions for Black Men.* Tallahasee, Florida: My Mind Productions & Assoc., Inc., 1991.

Abu-Jamal, Mumia. *Live From Death Row.* Reading: Addison Wesley, 1995.

Ali, Muhammad. *The Greatest.* New York: Random House, 1975.

Asante, M. *Afrocentricity.* Buffalo: Amulefi Publishing Company, 1980.

Ashe, Arthur R. *A Hard Road to Glory: A History of the African American Athlete 1619-1918, Vol. 1.* New York: Amistad, 1988.

Baldwin, James. *Nobody Knows My Name.* New York: Dial Press, 1961.

Barndt, Joseph. *Dismantling Racism.* Minneapolis: Augsburg Fortress, 1991.

Brietman, George. *Malcolm X Speaks.* New York: Grove Press, 1965.

Carroll, Charles. *The Negro a Beast.* St. Louis: Bible House Publishing Co., 1900.

Caute, David. *Frantz Fanon.* New York: Viking Press, 1970.

Chalmers, David M. *Hooded Americanism.* New York: New Viewpoints, 1951.

Chambers, Bradford, ed. *Chronicles of Negro Protest.* New York: Mentor Books, 1968.

Bibliography

Clarke, John Henrick. *Marcus Garvey and the Vision of Africa.* New York: Vintage Books, 1974.

———. *Malcolm X, The Man and His Times.* Trenton, New Jersey: Africa World Press, Inc., 1990.

———, ed. *Ten Black Writers Respond.* Boston: Beacon Press, 1968.

Curtis, Richard. *The Life of Malcolm X.* Philadelphia: Macrae Smith Company, 1971.

Diop, Cheikh Anta. *The African Origin of Civilization—Myth or Reality.* Westport: Publishers, Inc., U.S. Lawrence Hill & Co., 1974.

Dixon, Thomas, Jr. *The Clansman.* New York: A. Wessels Company, 1907.

———. *The Leopard's Spots.* New York: Grosset & Dunlap, 1902.

DuBois, W.E.B. *The Philadelphia Negro.* New York: Schocken Books, Inc., 1899/1967.

———. *In Battle for Peace.* New York: Schocken Books, Inc., 1952.

Ellison, Ralph. *Invisible Man.* New York: Random House, 1952.

Evanzz, Karl. *The Judas Factor—The Plot to Kill Malcolm X.* New York: Thunder Mouth Press, 1992.

Fanon, Frantz. *Black Skin White Masks.* New York: Grove Press, Inc., 1967.

———. *The Wretched of the Earth.* New York: Grove Press, Inc., 1963.

Faulkner, David. *Great Time Coming: The Life of Jackie Robinson From Baseball to Birmingham.* New York: Simon & Schuster, 1995.

Gary, Lawrence E., ed. *Black Men.* Beverly Hills, California: Sage, 1981.

Gossett, Thomas F. *Race: The History of an Idea in America.* New York: Schocken Books, 1965.

Grier, William H. and Price M. Cobbs. *Black Rage.* New York: Bantam Books, Inc., 1968.

Hacker, Andrew. *Two Nations: Black and White, Separate, Hostile, Unequal.* New York: Ballantine Books, 1992.

Hamilton, Virginia. *W.E.B. DuBois Autobiography*. New York: Thomas Y. Crowell, 1972.

Herrnstein, Richard and Charles Murray. *The Bell Curve: Intelligence and Class Structure in American Life*. New York: Simon & Schuster, 1994.

Hernton, Calvin C. *Sex and Racism in America*. New York: Double Day, 1965.

Higginbotham, A. Leon, Jr. *In the Matter of Color*. New York: Oxford University Press, 1978.

Jackson, George. *Soledad Brother: The Prison Letters of George Jackson*. New York: Bantham Books, 1970.

James, George, G. M. *Stolen Legacy*. San Francisco: Julian Richardson, Assoc., 1954.

Jones, Del. *Culture Bandits, Vol. 1*. Philadelphia, Pennsylvania: Hikeka Press, 1990.

Jordon, Winthrop D. *White Over Black*. Baltimore, Maryland: Penguin Books, 1968.

Leab, Daniel J. *From Sambo to Superspade*. Boston: Houghton Mifflin Company, 1965.

Louis, Joe with Edna & Art Rust, Jr. *Joe Louis, My Life*. New York: Harcourt Brace, 1978.

Madhabuti, Haki R. *Black Men, Obsolete, Single, Dangerous?* Chicago: Third World Press, 1990.

Malcolm X. *Malcolm X Talks To Young People*. New York: Pathfinder Press, 1965.

McIntyre, Charshee, C. L. *Criminalizing a Race*. New York: Kayode Publications, Ltd., 1992.

Newby, I.J. *Jim Crow's Defense*. Baton Rouge: Louisiana State University Press, 1965.

Patterson, William, L., ed. *We Charge Genocide*. New York: International Publishers, 1971.

Perry, Bruce. *Malcolm: The Life of a Man Who Changed Black America.* New York: Station Hill Press, Inc., 1991.

Powell, Adam Clayton, Jr. *Adam by Adam.* New York: Dial Press, 1971.

Robeson, Paul. *Here I Stand.* Boston: Beacon Press, 1958.

Rogers, J. A. *Sex and Race.* New York: J.A. Rogers Publications, 1941.

———. *Nature Knows No Color-Line.* New York: J.A. Rogers Publications, 1941.

Styron, William. *The Confessions of Nat Turner.* New York: Signet Books, 1966.

Van Sertima, Ivan. *Blacks in Science, Ancient and Modern.* New Brunswick: Transaction Books, 1988.

Weinstein, Allen and Frank O. Gatell. *American Negro Slavery.* New York: Oxford University Press, 1968.

Welsing, Frances Cress. *The Isis Papers.* Chicago: Third World Press, 1991.

Williams, Chancellor. *The Destruction of Black Civilization.* Chicago: Third World Press, 1991.

Wilson, Amos N. *Black on Black Violence.* New York: Afrikan World Info Systems, 1990.

Wolseley, Roland E. *The Black Press, U.S.A.* Ames: Iowa State University Press, 1971.

Yette, Samuel F. *The Choice: This Issue of Black Survival in America.* New York: G.P. Putnam's Sons, 1971.

MAGAZINES

Dreyfuss, Joel. "Why White Men Fear Black Men: White Men Tell the Truth." *Essence,* November 1992, 66-68, 70, 124, 126, 128, 130.

Fischel, Jack. "Strange 'Bell' Fellows." *Commonweal,* February 10, 1995, 16-17.

Jamison, Charles N., Jr. "Racism the Hurt That Men Won't Name." *Essence,* November 1992, 62-64, 122-123.

Ji-Ahnte Sibert, Anthony and Denise. "Medical Repression." *Z Magazine*, May 1994, 17-20.

Strickland, William. "The Future of Black Men." *Essence*, November 1989, 50-52, 110, 112, 114, 116.

Washington, Harriet A. "Human Guinea Pigs." *Emerge*, October 1994, 24-35.